N

VESUVIUS

AMPHITHEATER

Oplontis

Pompeii

Sarno River

Cover: Diana, goddess of the hunt, wears a poignant expression in this exquisite bronze sculpture from Pompeii's Temple of Apollo. The statue appears against a background of columns from a Pompeian garden, in a view looking north toward Mount Vesuvius, the city's destroyer.

End paper: Painted by the artist Paul Breeden on a surface specially textured to resemble vellum, the schematic map shows Vesuvius and its immediate environs before the fateful eruption of AD 79. Exaggerated views highlight a statue of Hercules at Herculaneum, a seaside villa at Oplontis, and the Amphitheater at Pompeii, which was actually situated in the city's southeast corner. Breeden also painted the vignettes illustrating the timeline on pages 160-161.

POMPEII:
THE VANISHED
CITY

LOST CIVILIZATIONS

The Consultants:
Wilhelmina F. Jashemski, professor emerita of ancient history at the University of Maryland, first visited Pompeii and Herculaneum in 1955 and has been studying the sites ever since. A renowned authority on Roman gardens, she served as consultant for the essay on the Garden of Hercules on pages 101-103 and reviewed portions of the text of chapter three, *The Pompeiians at Home.*

James Packer, professor of classics at Northwestern University, has excavated at Pompeii. He has written on such subjects as town planning and housing in Pompeii and has conducted a survey of the city's inns.

Robert W. Wallace is an assistant professor in the classics department at the Johns Hopkins University. He has written about the agriculture and economy of the ancient Roman world and about Hellenistic influences on Roman society. He has also conducted a study of the scrolls discovered at Herculaneum's Villa of the Papyri.

POMPEII: THE VANISHED CITY

By the Editors of Time-Life Books

TIME-LIFE BOOKS, ALEXANDRIA, VIRGINIA

CONTENTS

Bathed in the glow of a hazy sunset, Pompeii's Forum lies empty beneath the looming mass of Mount Vesuvius. In its day, the grand open space bustled with the comings and goings of the city's people. Reclaimed from the volcanic debris that entombed the city nearly 2,000 years ago, Pompeii today bears striking witness to the Roman way of life.

WHEN DARKNESS CAME ROLLING OVER THE LAND

Crouched and choking for air, a Pompeian mule driver encapsulates petrified time—August 25, AD 79. The rain of volcanic debris that buried the city preserved the shape of his body, enabling archaeologists to make this somber plaster cast of his final moment.

Late in August of 1991 the Roman city of Pompeii, already one of the world's most famous and fascinating archaeological sites, offered a fresh glimpse of the nightmare that had doomed it more than 1,900 years earlier. The excavators who made the discovery were not particularly looking for additional details of the tragic hours on August 24 and 25, AD 79, when the outpourings of nearby Mount Vesuvius overwhelmed the city. The diggers were to make repairs: They had received funding of $23 million from the Italian government to clear pebbly volcanic rubble called lapilli from several still-buried city blocks of Pompeii and restore the buildings underneath. But in the course of removing the rocky debris, they came upon a thick blanket of hardened ash, which inevitably turned their labors in a new direction.

At Pompeii, volcanic ash has been an archaeological boon, the cause of a sort of preservation miracle. During the latter phases of the eruption, it enveloped many of the victims and then solidified around them, leaving behind body-shaped cavities when the flesh decayed. From these molds—the first of which were discovered in the 1860s— experts have been able to produce scores of amazingly lifelike casts of Pompeii's unluckiest citizens. To the archaeologists on the 1991 dig, the newfound ash layer seemed a possible source of more figures of the dead. It was worth a try.

Using a recently invented technique designed to keep casts from shrinking as they harden, workers pumped a viscous mixture of cement and bauxite into likely-looking cracks and crevices in the solid ash. They gave it several weeks to dry, then began chipping away the ash covering to see if any secrets lay within. A macabre tableau emerged—the casts of nine people caught in a moment of horror.

What had happened to these people was all too clear. For some time, they had huddled in a ground-floor room of a house as rocky particles poured down on the city, piling up on roofs, rising in the streets, pressing through any doorway or window that offered an opening. Gradually the tide of lapilli had filled the room to a depth of about eight feet. Atop the pile, the group waited for the rain of rock to stop, and finally it did. Perhaps, with a rush of relief, they thought that the eruption was over, that they had been spared. Then suddenly, sweeping down on the city like the very breath of death, came a hot cloud of ash and gas. Choking, panicked, they lunged toward the doorway. It was hopeless. The poisonous gas snuffed out their lives before they could move more than a few feet.

Now, under an August sun in another age, the scene lay bared, almost photographically fixed by the casts. The victims—men, women, two children—were strewn on their rocky deathbed, some face-down, some on their backs. One man was resting on his elbow, trying to lift his head; one was tucked in a kind of fetal position; one was gesturing toward a fellow victim. One was a woman in late pregnancy. Perhaps that was her husband beside her, stretching out the edge of his garment to shield her from the hot ash, the imprint of the cloth still visible on her face.

For excavators at Pompeii, it was a familiar sight, but one that has never lost its wrenching power. Pompeii today is a necropolis, a city of the dead, as is the smaller town of Herculaneum lying less than 10 miles to the northwest, which also succumbed to Vesuvius. In addition, the killing hand of the volcano fell across numerous country villas in the area, from the estates of Boscoreale on the mountain's lower slopes belonging to the wealthy to the shoreline dwellings of Oplontis and Stabiae.

Only a few days' journey from Rome by coach, these communities clustered around the Bay of Naples were far from obscure. Pompeii boasted on the order of 20,000 residents; Herculaneum—a quiet suburb of the much-larger Neapolis (modern-day Naples), just three or four miles to the north—had a more modest population of

In 1991, workers excavating a residence in Pompeii came upon this group of men, women, and children—preserved now in the form of casts made by archaeologists—who died moments after poisonous fumes swept down from Mount Vesuvius. In the foreground of the scene, a man vainly attempts to shield the face of a woman who is about seven months pregnant.

perhaps five thousand. But what truly sets these places apart and makes them such an archaeological marvel is the abruptness with which they were snatched from the realm of the living. In a brief and dreadful spasm of violence, the volcano smothered them under countless tons of rock and ash, submerging Pompeii to a maximum depth of about 25 feet and burying Herculaneum in a stony-hard volcanic matrix that in places is 65 feet thick.

By sealing away the area so completely, Vesuvius in effect stopped time. One day the cities were bubbling with vitality, the houses alive with domestic doings, the streets full of movement and talk, the taverns and baths cheerfully serving a populace that knew how to enjoy itself. In a stroke it was all gone; the life extinguished, the buildings and byways and all the complex machinery of a flourishing society vanished from the face of the earth.

The rediscovery of Pompeii and other ruins nearby is one of archaeology's greatest stories. From the subterranean sepulchers has come not only an extraordinary narrative of disaster but also a uniquely detailed and comprehensive picture of private and public life in the classical world. Paintings and mosaics have survived to shed new light on the values, beliefs, and everyday workings of Roman culture. The give-and-take of politics can be traced in graffiti and proclamations on Pompeian walls. The operations of bakeries, tanneries, and wool-working shops can be discerned. The plants in gardens can be identified. Food that people ate has been recovered. Even such intimate matters as sexual practices are revealed by evidence in the ruins. (As one student of Herculaneum has expressed it, none of the volcano's victims was able "to put up a false front, tidying rooms normally in disorder, or changing the pictures and statuary to avoid shocking our Puritan sense of propriety.") It was the destiny of Pompeii and Herculaneum to speak to the future with unsurpassed clarity—a destiny that required a terrible doom.

Although Pompeii and its smaller neighbors ended in horror, they began in bright promise. Few places are more bountifully endowed than the Bay of Naples. The well-watered coastal plain, enriched by the minerals of volcanic ash, is among the most fertile regions of the Italian Peninsula, capable of bearing three or more crops a year. The climate is gentle, with brief winters, long springs and autumns, and summers kept temperate by sea breezes. The bay offers excellent anchorage and a fine harvest for fishermen. Pompeii itself sits just south of Vesuvius, about half a mile from the coast on the Sarno River, which serves as a highway to the interior.

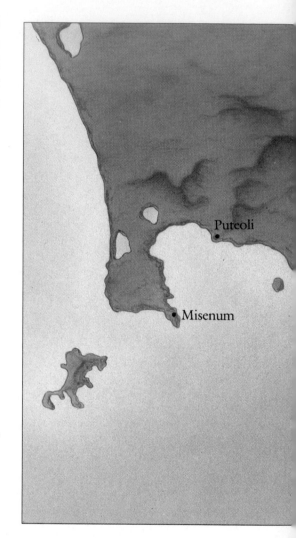

The earliest known inhabitants of the region were a tribal group who spoke a language called Oscan. They raised cattle, farmed, and by the beginning of the first millennium BC had dotted the area with villages. Sometime in the seventh century BC, newcomers appeared. The Greeks, a restless people, were then spreading all around the shores of the Mediterranean and the Black Sea, and they found this particular corner of the world irresistible. It was they who established Neapolis, the "New City," as a center of trade in the area, building on the roots of a much-older community. But they also left their mark on the smaller towns that had arisen along the curving fringe of the bay, Pompeii among them. About 200 years later, the Greeks lost political control to the Samnites, a collection of belligerent clans from the hilly interior. Then, in the last years of the fourth century BC, an aggressive and disciplined people from a fast-growing city-state to the north defeated the Samnites, and the era of Roman dominion began.

Within the next 200 years or so, Pompeii became a full-fledged city, grown sevenfold since Greek times, from 23 acres to 160 acres, with walls almost two miles around. Its citizens were proud and feisty—and ever reluctant to bend to Roman rule. In 91 BC, Pompeii and Herculaneum joined a peninsula-wide rebellion that was suppressed in the Vesuvian region by Lucius Cornelius Sulla, a general who would later become dictator of Rome. Fighting broke out again 18 years later when an escaped gladiator named Spartacus, soon to lead a great slave uprising, took refuge with 70 fellow rebels on the summit of Vesuvius. As Roman soldiers closed in for the kill, the fugitives used vines to climb down a supposedly impassable cliff, then routed their pursuers. A gifted and inspiring military leader, Spartacus defied the hated Roman overlords for another two years before finally dying in battle.

Despite the occasional political storms, the region continued to flourish, becoming something of a playground for the rich. On hillsides that overlooked the sparkling bay, Rome's wealthiest and

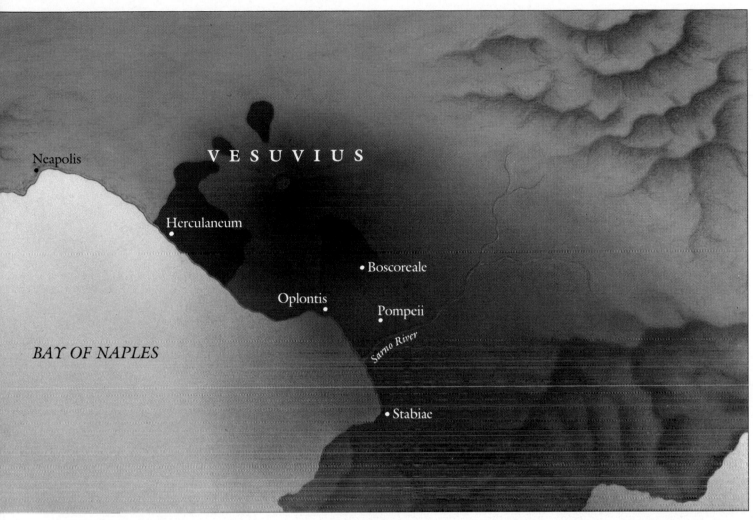

VESUVIUS

Neapolis

Herculaneum

• Boscoreale

Oplontis

Pompeii

Sarno River

BAY OF NAPLES

• Stabiae

The power of Vesuvius to bury its near neighbors took two main forms, as is shown in this schematic view of the Bay of Naples and its surroundings. Wind-borne ash and pumice—represented by varying densities of gray—blanketed the entire region to the south. Flows of denser volcanic debris (red) obliterated Herculaneum to the west, as well as creeping over other areas in thinner layers.

noblest families built country houses—gleaming showplaces of luxury, some with 50 rooms or more. The great statesman and orator Cicero had three properties in the neighborhood; the son-in-law of the emperor Augustus owned a villa; a son of the future emperor Claudius choked to death on a pear in a country house at Pompeii; the emperor Tiberius may have owned a large villa near Herculaneum in addition to his sumptuous estate on the island of Capri at the bay's southern tip.

While ease and pleasure were very much in the air, the hum of business was always audible. From the evidence uncovered along its shorefront, Herculaneum was apparently devoted to fishing rather than to trade. Pompeii was considerably more commercial and dynamic. In addition to its role as a trading link between the Italian interior and the wider world, it was a regional center for cloth making

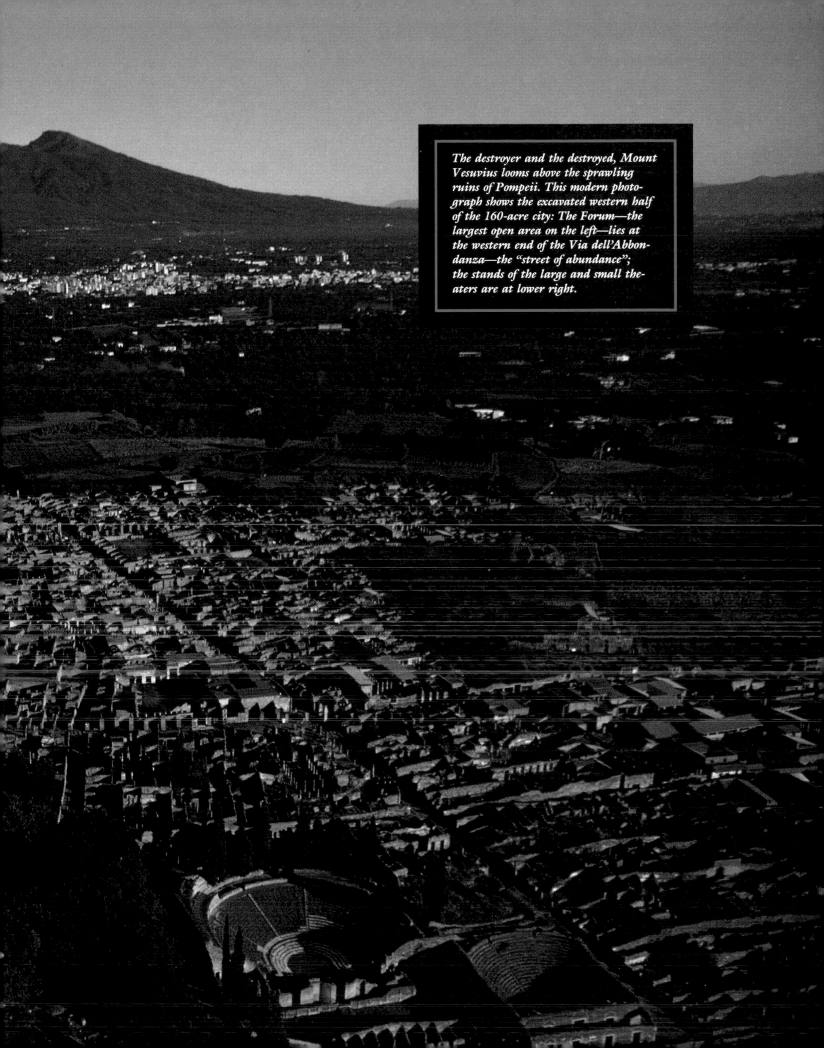

The destroyer and the destroyed, Mount Vesuvius looms above the sprawling ruins of Pompeii. This modern photograph shows the excavated western half of the 160-acre city: The Forum—the largest open area on the left—lies at the western end of the Via dell'Abbondanza—the "street of abundance"; the stands of the large and small theaters are at lower right.

and dyeing, and a home for scores of artisans—metalworkers, potters, glassblowers, and others. Vestiges of earlier cultures survived, but Roman ways—especially in politics and civic administration—predominated. Among other amenities, the city had a large amphitheater for gladiatorial games; built by a Roman speculator, it could hold 20,000 people. Two theaters offered plays and musical entertainment for the amusement of the population. More than a hundred bars and taverns dispensed refreshment. Three working public baths (a fourth was under construction at the time of the eruption) provided venues for relaxation and socializing. At least seven brothels, unabashedly erotic in their decor, supplied other sorts of pleasures. In addition, Pompeii boasted at least 10 temples and, next to the large open space of the Forum, a grand basilica that served as a combination law court, bank, and meeting place for businessmen.

The streets of the city were paved with volcanic stone. Gutters ran alongside them, carrying away sewage and other filth; lead pipes buried just beneath the surface brought in fresh water. Fountains, a few made of marble and fitted with ornate spouts, supplied drinking water to people and animals passing through the streets. Dwellings ranged from extensive, lavishly decorated houses with courtyards and gardens to humble second- or third-story apartments or simple rooms behind shops.

Thus, then, was Pompeii as the empire of Augustus Caesar and his immediate successors began its reign of power. It was, to be sure, a provincial city, but could still count itself an admirable reflection of Roman ambitions, a worthy example of a culture that—with heavy borrowings from the Greeks—had remade the earth. Comfortable and confident, Pompeii and its neighbors had no real worries in the middle years of the first century AD. But their nemesis had been present all along. Over them loomed the brooding volcano, singed by ancient fires, and now beginning to stir again after centuries of sleep.

Picturing the collapse of a monumental arch (left) and the Temple of Jupiter (center) in the Forum, a marble relief from a Pompeian household altar commemorates the earthquake of AD 62—an unrecognized warning of far-greater devastation to come. In a touch of humor, the rider atop the equestrian statue beside the temple is shown losing his balance. The scenes at right include an altar to Tellus (earth) and a bull being prepared for sacrifice.

Vesuvius had concealed its nature well. Rising to a height of only about 6,000 feet, the mountain had given no clear sign of threatening behavior through all of recorded history. Its upper slopes were sometimes warm, but this was hardly considered ominous; few people were even aware that it was a volcano. It was cloaked in green, with pastures and orchards and vineyards spreading up its sides, and game-rich woods near the summit. Understandably enough, no legend or folk tale warned of its darker side: In AD 79, the volcano had not erupted in more than a thousand years.

But all that while, tremendous geological stresses had been building up as, at the rate of about an inch a year, two drifting blocks of the earth's crust—tectonic plates—ground together in a titanic slow-motion collision that began deep in the past and will continue far into the future. One plate carries the continent of Africa, the other Eurasia, and their collision is forcing the edge of the floor of the Mediterranean Sea down into the bowels of the planet. This tectonic action created Vesuvius and a string of other active volcanoes along Italy's west coast, including Ischia, Vulcano, Vulcanello, Stromboli, and Sicily's towering Etna. It also accounts for the frequent tremors in this part of the world.

In AD 62, the sudden release of pent-up stresses caused the earth to shiver violently. The quake's epicenter was very close to Pompeii, and as the ground heaved, the system of pipes that delivered water to the city was ripped apart. Many villas and smaller houses collapsed, burying people in the ruins. Even worse hit were public buildings, which were constructed of heavier materials and thus less able to ride out the earthquake. "Six hundred sheep were swallowed by the earth," reported the essayist Seneca. "Statues were thrown from their pedestals and smashed, people wandered about completely out of their senses."

The damage was so extensive that Nero, the emperor at the time, wondered whether it might not be better just to abandon the place. But the inhabitants did what they could to get Pompeii back on its feet, and 17 years later they were still hard at work, trying to restore such structures as the Basilica to their former glory.

No one, it seems, associated the earthquake with Vesuvius. The mountain's green bulk remained silent as masons and carpenters

As plumes of fire and clouds of ash fill the sky, Pliny the Elder collapses on the shores of Stabiae in this 1813 painting by Pierre-Henri de Valenciennes. The historian and naval commander died rescuing others from the volcanic inferno.

and engineers kept busy below. But the destructive rumbling had been a preamble, a twitch that signaled the approaching end of the volcano's long repose.

Early in August of AD 79, tremors again shook the countryside around Vesuvius. At the same time, a number of wells dried up and springs ceased to flow—symptoms of pressure rising in the earth. On the 20th day of the month, a moderate shock rippled through the area. Horses and cattle appeared excited and frightened; birds grew strangely quiet. Some people, remembering the quake of 62, gathered their belongings and left for safer ground. They were none too soon. During the night of August 23 or the early morning of the 24th, ash began to issue from the volcano, lightly dusting the land downwind. Whatever was happening still seemed fairly innocuous. But about 1:00 p.m., the monster threw off its last restraints.

With a stupendous crack, the floor of the crater—the plug of solidified lava that had long sealed the volcano's throat—gave way under pressure and was blown to fragments, transforming Vesuvius into a giant cannon, its muzzle open to the sky. Molten rock shot 17 miles into the stratosphere, traveling at approximately twice the speed of sound. Shredded into small particles as it flew upward, it eventually lost momentum, spread out in a flat cloud, and was blown to the southeast by stratospheric winds. Pompeii and Stabiae lay in that direction, and the debris started to rain down on them.

Nineteen miles away, at the naval base of Misenum across the bay, a startled youth watched the eruption. This 17-year-old lad, known to history as Pliny the Younger, had come to Misenum with his mother to visit his uncle, Pliny the Elder, one of the great men of the Roman Empire—author of a 37-volume encyclopedia of natural history and admiral of a Roman fleet. Like his infinitely curious uncle, the young man would prove a gifted observer, subsequently writing a vivid eyewitness account of the disaster at the request of the historian Tacitus.

Of this first phase of the eruption, he noted that the cloud "resembled a pine tree, for it shot up at a great height in the form of a trunk, which extended itself at the top into several branches. It was at one moment white, at another dark and spotted, as if it had carried up earth and cinders. My uncle, true savant that he was, deemed the phenomenon important and worth a nearer view. He ordered a light vessel to be got ready." A little later, Pliny the Elder received a note indicating that people close to the eruption were in peril. Setting aside his first impulse to observe the event as a scientist, he mounted a rescue mission, leading several large galleys across the bay. His nephew was not aboard—he said he had to stay home and study—but reconstructed the scene from reports collected afterward. "And now cinders, which grew thicker and hotter the nearer he approached, fell into the ships, then pumice stones, too, with stones blackened, scorched, and cracked by fire. Then the sea ebbed suddenly from under them, while the shore was blocked up by landslips from the mountains." The captain of Pliny's galley urged a retreat, but the admiral ordered him to press on to Stabiae. The decision would prove to be his undoing.

Meanwhile, the coast and hills southeast of the mountain had become an arena of bewilderment and fear. As high-altitude winds steered the great cloud overhead, Pompeii and the country villas nearby were wrapped in darkness. From the sky came an endless rocky downpour—some of the particles no bigger than rice grains, others fist-sized. Although the deluge consisted mostly of pumice, a lightweight rock made porous by expanding gases, about 10 percent of the fall was dense stone. Hurtling down at high speed, the heavier projectiles claimed a number of lives.

Within two or three hours, Pompeii was a foot or so deep in pebbly pumice and stone. Buildings began to collapse, causing more deaths: People were crushed as roofs gave way or were struck down in the streets as walls crumbled and columns fell. Fires broke out as lamps shattered and spilled their oil.

During the early hours of the eruption, most of the population fled—by boat, horse, or mule, in chariots, and on foot. But at least 2,000 people elected to stay, either intimidated by what was going on or because they were unwilling to abandon their homes and businesses. They scrambled about on the rising drifts of pumice or huddled under roofs that held firm under the growing load of rock. All through the afternoon and evening, the volcano continued to spew its grapeshot of rock high into the stratosphere. As the particles drifted downwind and descended to earth, Pompeii's burden of pumice grew at an astounding rate—approximately six inches every hour.

Produced with uncompromising realism, this bronze head unearthed in 1754 from a villa at Herculaneum was among the early prizes looted from the site. Long thought to represent the Roman philosopher Seneca, the face is more likely that of an anonymous actor, the Greek poet Hesiod, or perhaps the Latin epic poet Ennius.

Expressing the romance attendant upon the discovery of Herculaneum, this 18th-century engraving is nevertheless inaccurate. It shows excavators bringing the city to light; in reality they tunneled through the 65-foot-thick hardened volcanic matrix. The items lined up in the foreground, though, reflect the passion of the day: collecting antiquities.

So far, Herculaneum had been largely spared the rain of pumice. Nonetheless, many of its inhabitants apparently left. Night fell, lit by the play of lightning around the column billowing skyward. The scene was spectacular, hypnotic from the close vantage of those who remained in the town. But the watchers were in mortal peril. Soon the volcano would demonstrate a new way to kill, and Herculaneum would be hit first.

At about one o'clock on the morning of August 25, as pressure in the volcano's throat briefly abated, the massive column collapsed, sending a glowing cascade of material down the sides of the mountain. The avalanche quickly separated into two waves. One was a hot, turbulent, fast-moving cloud of lightweight ash and gases. The other consisted of a denser, slower, ground-hugging flow of pumice

This gold ring from Pompeii, bearing an image of a comic theater mask, once graced the hand of King Charles III of Spain, who reigned over the Vesuvian region for a time during the 1700s— and appropriated some of the valuables uncovered by the excavations.

and larger rock fragments mixed with soil from the slopes and made fluid by temperatures as high as 750 degrees Fahrenheit. The front-running ash cloud probably descended at a rate of at least 100 miles per hour, taking no more than four minutes to reach Herculaneum and giving those below fruitless seconds to dash in panic toward the sea. Roaring through the city, it ripped off roof tiles, knocked stones askew, and caused the sea to boil when it reached the waterfront. It scorched flesh and filled lungs with ash, searing and asphyxiating every human and animal in its path. Not one living creature survived. A few moments later, the great tide of denser debris flooded in, rolling down the streets, pouring through the doorways of houses and public buildings, reshaping the shore.

Herculaneum was utterly dead, and the volcano now proceeded to bury it in a deep grave. Again and again over the ensuing hours—six times in all—Vesuvius belched violently and sent an ash cloud and a trailing wave of rock down on the little seaport, until the buildings lay lost somewhere in the depths of an unrecognizable world. Pompeii, farther from the maw, escaped these avalanches at first, just as Herculaneum had escaped the rocky rain. But Vesuvius was still gaining strength, and at about 7:30 a.m., with the fourth surge, the volcano took deadly aim at the city beside the Sarno. A hot cloud of ash and gas raced across the now-blackened fields, swept through Pompeii, and asphyxiated every person it reached.

A fifth surge followed minutes later. Then, at about 8:00 a.m., came the sixth and most powerful avalanche of all. At that hour, Pliny the Elder had emerged from a villa at Stabiae, where he had somehow managed to sleep through the night. As his nephew later wrote, the admiral and some companions "thought it proper to go down upon the shore to observe from close at hand if they could possibly put out to sea, but they found that the waves still ran extremely high and contrary. There, my uncle, having thrown himself down upon a disused sail, repeatedly called for and drank draughts of cold water; soon after, flames and a strong smell of sulfur dispersed the rest of the company in flight." Pliny the Elder, who was quite corpulent and had a history of respiratory problems, could not summon the strength to follow: "He raised himself up with the assistance of two of his slaves, but instantly fell." His nephew conjectured that the fumes had overwhelmed him, but since the others did not succumb, a heart attack seems more likely. In any event, the great man was dead.

In Misenum on the other side of the bay, Pliny the Younger

had been awake for hours, alarmed by a series of powerful tremors. When the house threatened to collapse, he and his mother joined a large crowd fleeing the town. "The coaches that we had ordered out, though upon the most level ground, were sliding to and fro and could not be kept steady even when stones were put against the wheels. Then we beheld the sea sucked back, leaving many sea animals captive on the dry sand."

More terrifying still was the sight of the volcano, working up to its ultimate paroxysm. "A black and dreadful cloud bursting out in gusts of igneous serpentine vapor now and again yawned open to reveal long, fantastic flames, resembling flashes of lightning but much larger. Soon afterward, the cloud began to descend upon the earth and cover the sea. Ashes now fell upon us, though as yet in no great quantity. I looked behind me; darkness came rolling over the land after us like a torrent. I proposed, while we yet could see, to turn aside, lest we should be knocked down in the road by a crowd that followed us, and trampled to death in the dark. We had scarce sat down when darkness overspread us, not like that of a moonless or cloudy night, but of a room when it is shut up and the lamp put out. You could hear the shrieks of women and crying children and the shouts of men; some were seeking their children, others their parents; some praying to die, from the very fear of dying; many lifting their hands to the gods; but the greater part imagining that there were no gods left anywhere, that the last and eternal night was come upon the world."

Because the cloud had to travel so far to reach Miscnum, it thinned and cooled, leaving Pliny the Younger and his mother unscathed. But it harmed them in another way: This was the same surge that had killed Pliny the Elder at Stabiae.

By now Vesuvius had been erupting for almost 18 hours. At last it began to weaken, although ash continued to sift down on the area for several more days. A great deal of Pompeii, like Herculaneum, had already disappeared from view. The volcano's coda of ash discharges covered nearly everything that remained, drawing a veil over the city's final agony.

Perhaps as much as 90 percent of Pompeii's population had left in time. Many people returned in the ensuing days and weeks, grieving as they scanned the desertlike hillside where the city had stood. Some started to dig. Locating their houses by whatever jutted above the surface, men tunneled shafts down into the ash and vol-

Cupids harvesting and pressing grapes adorn a wine amphora found in a tomb outside the Herculaneum Gate of Pompeii. With opaque white images on a translucent background, the rare cameo glass vase, too sophisticated to have been made locally, undoubtedly proclaimed the wealth and prestige of its owner.

canic pebbles, then burrowed sideways, breaking through walls as they went from room to room. They managed to extract many of their valuables—and most likely also removed much that did not belong to them. Archaeologists would later come across buildings that had been stripped of statues, marble veneer on walls, and other ornamentation.

At one mansion, diggers had worked in apparently random fashion through the rooms surrounding the peristyle, or garden courtyard; their plundering may have succeeded, but they missed a cache of valuables in the house next-door—an elaborate silver table service and a collection of gold jewelry. Disaster attended some of the efforts. Poison gas trapped under the ash took a toll, and a number of tunnels caved in, adding to the city's dead. The dangerous searching was soon abandoned.

Despite the obvious completeness of the devastation, some thought was given to rebuilding Pompeii. The Roman emperor at the time was Titus, who had come to power only two months before Vesuvius went on its rampage. Appalled by reports of the calamity, he appointed a commission of senators to study remedial measures. He also encouraged unharmed towns in the area to help refugees. By his instruction, the property of those who had died without heirs was assigned to the cause of relief. But the job of disinterring Pompeii was simply too big, and reconstruction plans were set aside. As for Herculaneum, it was hopelessly out of reach.

The land did not remain entirely vacant: A few farmers' huts appeared on the hill overlooking the Sarno, and a village grew up atop the entombed Herculaneum. Stabiae recovered sufficiently to take over Pompeii's trading business. But all this was a far cry from what had been there before, and memories of past glory soon faded. Looking ahead, the poet Statius posed a rhetorical question: "Will future centuries, when new seed will have covered over the waste, believe that entire cities and their inhabitants lie under their feet, and that the fields of their ancestors were drowned in a sea of flames?" The answer turned out to be mixed: People forgot the cities, but not the power of Vesuvius.

The volcano would not let them forget. In AD 202, it erupted for a week. Other major convulsions occurred in 306, 472, 513, 533,

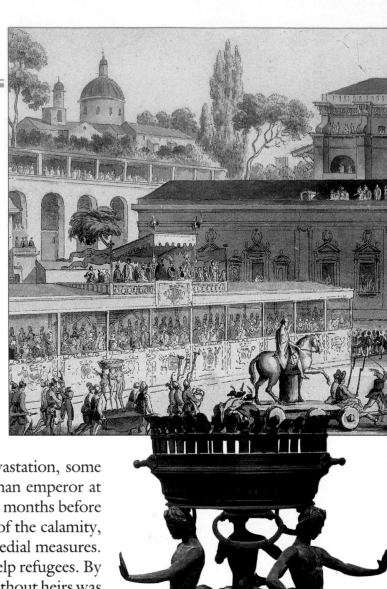

With all the pomp of a victory parade, special wagons bear precious Pompeian and Herculanean artifacts in 1787 to safekeeping in the newly refurbished Naples Museum. This engraving by Francesco Piranesi and Jean-Louis Desprez shows actual pieces conveyed that day, including a bronze charcoal brazier supported by three satyrs (left) that came from a Herculaneun villa probably owned by Julius Caesar's father-in-law, and a bronze horse (above) that once stood with a full chariot entourage at the entrance to Herculaneum's Basilica.

and, after a millennium of relative quiescence, in 1631. Of this series, the last was the worst, almost as violent as the eruption of 79. Seven streams of lava issued from the crater and poured down the slopes, destroying almost all the towns at the foot of the volcano. As many as 18,000 people may have been killed.

By the time of Vesuvius' 17th-century outburst, Pompeii and Herculaneum had almost completely slipped from memory. Their rediscovery proceeded not from any intentional search for the lost cities but from a foreigner's acquisitive impulse. In 1707, as a result of a minor move on the chessboard of European politics, Sicily and the portion of southern Italy centering on Naples became Austrian territory, and a titled general, Prince d'Elboeuf, arrived to serve as local commander of the cavalry. The assignment was thoroughly agreeable to the prince, not just because of the pleasant climate and sun-splashed beauty of the Bay of Naples but also because the region had a strong connection with the classical age. From the Renaissance onward, cultivated Europeans had regarded the days of ancient Greece and Rome as a finer era than their own—indeed, as the noblest chapter in human history. Finding himself on hallowed ground, Prince d'Elboeuf decided to build a villa and decorate it with mementos of antiquity.

Vases, fragments of columns or bas-reliefs, bits of statuary, and other vestiges of Roman times were occasionally recovered from the hills and fields by peasants and could be purchased for a suitable sum. But the prince got wind of a better source. Learning that a new well being sunk in the garden of a monastery at the foot of Vesuvius had turned up some exceptional objects, he promptly bought the land and set a crew to the task of digging laterally from the bottom of the well shaft. The workers soon hauled up three magnificent statues of draped females, along with fragments of a statue of Hercules and numerous other interesting items. The well, it seemed, was a relic hunter's bull's-eye, a lucky thrust that had apparently hit some sort of richly adorned public edifice.

D'Elboeuf believed that they had come upon a temple, no doubt part of a community. The reality would have staggered him. All around the structure, sealed under 50 to 65 feet of rock-hard volcanic matter, with the village of Resina perched on the surface, were the streets and houses and shops and civic buildings of what had been an ancient seaport.

After the prince had looted the place of all its statuary, his interest waned, but he had set a treasure hunt in motion. A few decades later, when another twist in the power arrangements of Europe brought the area under Spanish control, quarrying at the site of the well picked up again. The new proprietor, King Charles III, assigned the duty to his Royal Engineers, led by the Cavaliere Rocco de Alcubierre. On December 11, 1738, the diggers found an inscription that bore the words *Theatrum Herculanensi*. The building mined by d'Elboeuf now had an identity: It was a theater rather than a temple. And its community had a name. This was Herculaneum.

Although the little city on the bay had been largely forgotten, a few historians knew of its existence—and its fate—from ancient literary references. The poet Martial, who was born in Spain but made his fame in Rome, had memorialized the port in ornate phrases: "Behold Vesuvius, once covered with green vineyards, producers of fruity wines: This is the mount that Bacchus loved better even than the hills of Nysa and on which the satyrs wove their dances. And here was Herculaneum, which vaunted the name of the hero Hercules. Everything lies under the flames and glowing ashes."

Even in academic circles, however, the precise location of the seaside town had remained unknown, primarily because the thick flow of volcanic debris that poured over the area had entirely altered the shoreline, extending it outward into the Bay of Naples by at least several hundred yards. But the theater's inscription solved the mystery: Herculaneum was about four and a half miles southwest of the summit of Vesuvius.

Similar uncertainties applied to Pompeii, which was also commemorated in classical documents. Scholars were aware that it lay to the southeast of the volcano, but no one could say exactly where. One interesting possibility, in the opinion of a few, was a spur of the mountain overlooking the Sarno River, about six miles from the crater. For centuries, the bones of some ancient buildings had protruded from a hillside there. Among the local populace, the spot was called La Civita—a modern version of the Latin word *civitas,* or city.

In 1762, the Prussian-born scholar Johann Joachim Winckelmann, shown here in a contemporary painting, published the first objective account of antiquities discovered around Vesuvius. Two years later, he revolutionized the fledgling science of archaeology with his groundbreaking History of the Art of Antiquity, *the first attempt ever to understand an ancient culture through its artifacts.*

In 1594, workmen digging an underground channel to bring water to a new villa nearby at the village of Torre Annunziata had found a stone bearing the inscription *decurio Pompeiis*. The general assumption was that it referred to the Roman statesman Pompey the Great and was just another of the many random relics so common throughout the Italian countryside. The discovery was, for all intents and purposes, ignored.

The truth did not emerge until the middle of the 18th century. In 1748, the team of Spanish engineers who had been laboring at Herculaneum since the previous decade turned their attention to La Civita, lured by reports of the discovery of antiquities. They soon hit paydirt, first exhuming a beautiful wall painting of fruits and flowers, then a man's skeleton with bronze and silver coins scattered beside the bones. With what little money he could gather, the man had evidently been running from the volcano's lethal fallout.

The Spanish excavators, however, had little interest in human drama; they cared only about marbles and other such classical trophies. At this new site, the quarrying work was much less demanding than at Herculaneum because the covering of debris was looser and far shallower. Still, the identity of La Civita remained uncertain until August of 1763, when workers came upon an inscription that included the words *res publica Pompeianorum*—"the commonwealth of Pompeians." The ancient city had been found.

All through this period, the treasure hunt continued at a rapid pace, in the process inflicting a good deal of damage on the priceless Vesuvian trove. Alcubierre, the engineer who was in charge of the excavations from 1738 until 1765, was little better than a looter. In his eagerness to acquire fresh prizes for Spain's Charles III, he scurried from one site to another, digging shafts and tunnels willy-nilly, abandoning any hole that did not pay off at once, ransacking any house or temple he encountered. Frescoes were cut away from their walls. Vases, coins, statues, and other articles were scooped up with no attempt to record where they had been found. Blasts of gunpowder speeded the plunder.

The crude techniques worked well enough: King Charles's growing collection of antiquities was the envy of Europe. Occasionally, notable visitors to the area got a chance to share in the thrill of discovery. As a guest surveyed the digs with an admiring eye, a

Giuseppe Fiorelli, appointed director of Pompeian excavations in 1860, ushered archaeological practices in the Vesuvian area into the modern age. In addition to mapping the city and imposing a system on the digging, Fiorelli made the first plaster casts of bodies buried under the volcano's ash and debris.

workman would give an exultant cry and hold up some treasure that had supposedly just surfaced—but that had in fact been planted there as a ready-made find.

In time, scholars gained a say in the proceedings. The year 1755 saw the formation of the Academy of Herculaneum, which devoted itself to printing a series of volumes on the artifacts recovered from the city. A brilliant German antiquarian named Johann Winckelmann, later to be called the father of archaeology, visited the Vesuvian digs and in the 1760s published descriptions of what was turning up in Herculaneum. He was the first to conduct an organized study of retrieved objects—and the first to realize how valuable such an approach could be in understanding the world of the ancients.

An even more famous German, the writer-scientist Johann Wolfgang von Goethe, arrived in 1787 to examine the remains of the two cities. He was particularly appalled by the methods of Alcubierre, writing some years later, "A thousand pities that the excavation had not been carried out in an orderly manner by German miners, since, without doubt, in the course of a haphazard predatory grubbing about, many noble antiquities were wastefully dispersed." Yet he too was captivated by the magnificent cache of relics being unearthed, almost losing sight of the great tragedy that attended their interment: "Many a calamity has happened to the world, but never one that has caused so much entertainment to posterity as this one."

The region again changed hands in 1798, when Napoleon added it to France's territory. Ten years later, after he had been crowned emperor, he installed a handpicked royal couple in Naples to look after his interests: Marshal of France Joachim Murat and his wife, Caroline, Napoleon's sister. Under their enthusiastic guidance, the pace of excavation accelerated. At least 500 workmen labored at the diggings. Queen Caroline in particular found the process enthralling—not just because of the recovery of jewelry or artworks but also because of the emergence of skeletons that gave a human dimension to the buried cities. Taking frequent leave from her court duties at Naples, she wandered about the sites, barraging project supervisors with questions about their work. Eventually she became so obsessed with the ruins that she had an apartment built nearby.

For many years, there continued to be an air more of plunder than of serious inquiry to the excavations around Vesuvius. A genuine effort to investigate the past did not emerge until after the formation

RESURRECTING A LONG-BURIED CITY

To their discoverers, Pompeii and Herculaneum suggested only devastation, sites to be raided, not explored. Even the renowned German art historian Johann Winckelmann derided the idea of excavating them. "Where would be the gain," he wrote in 1784, "since all that would come to light of the houses crushed between huge masses of lava would be the shattered walls?"

For the next century, this way of thinking more or less prevailed. But then, in 1860, the appointment of Giuseppe Fiorelli as director of Pompeian excavations changed things forever. Recognizing the unparalleled insights that could be gained into the Roman past by careful study of the ruins and all that they contained, Fiorelli set as his goal the total recovery of the vanished city.

A pioneer of modern archaeological methods, Fiorelli instituted a policy of completely clearing one site before moving on to the next, taking pains to excavate the areas between them as well. As Pompeii's streets, houses, and defensive walls and gates began to emerge, Fiorelli was able to divide the city into regions and blocks and develop a plan for its systematic disengagement from the 10 to 20 feet of volcanic debris.

As the digging proceeded, one of Fiorelli's guiding principles was that new finds—from frescoes to furniture—be left in place whenever possible to preserve their ancient context. His journals recorded his progress and set a standard that has enabled Pompeii's subsequent excavators to go on breathing life into the past.

Two images from the mid-1890s reflect excavation practices devised by Giuseppe Fiorelli three decades earlier. At right, laborers haul debris from a dig that features a fresco Fiorelli let stay in place. Below, workers reconstruct walls of the House of the Vettii.

Fiorelli's vision of a restored Pompeii encompassed far more work than could be realized in his lifetime, but his successors took up both his goal and his disciplined methods of excavation. Foremost among them was an archaeologist named Vittorio Spinazzola. From 1910 to 1923, Spinazzola oversaw an ambitious project to uncover the nearly 3,000-foot-long Via dell'Abbondanza, Pompeii's main shopping street. Under his guid-ance, the thoroughfare and the buildings lining it began to take on some of their appearance before the eruption.

Following a technique pioneered by Fiorelli, Spinazzola first drilled down to establish the route of the Via dell'Abbondanza, then began digging out the structures from above. After removing the debris, he protected any furnishings or frescoes found within buildings and then shored up the walls to prevent them from collapsing when the street itself was cleared.

Like Fiorelli, Spinazzola insisted that all objects uncovered be left where they were found. In particular, he made certain that not only interior wall paintings but also the colorful shop signs, election notices, and graffiti adorning exterior walls were carefully preserved, to project the city's history.

One of Spinazzola's outstanding contributions to the restora-

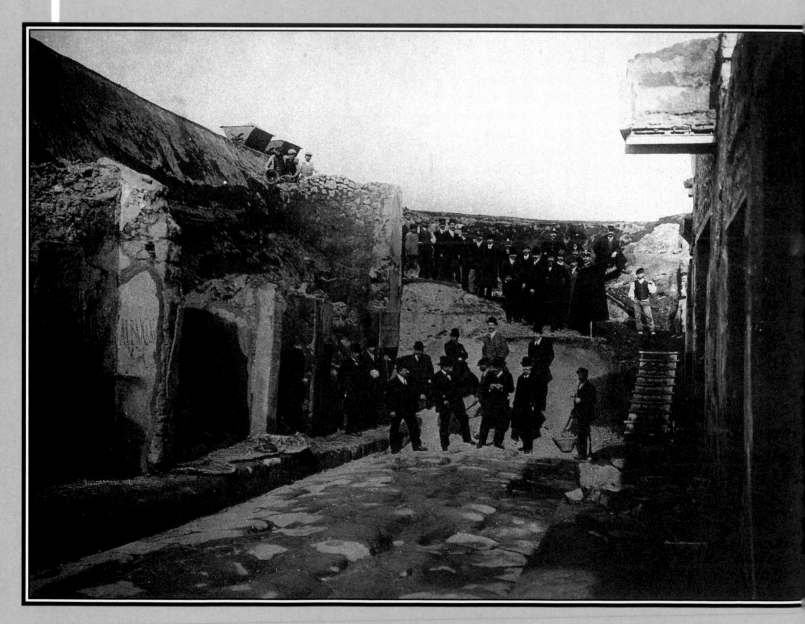

tion of Pompeii was his meticulous reconstruction of the upper stories, windows, balconies, and roofs of buildings lining the Via dell'Abbondanza *(opposite, below)*. He was also one of the first archaeologists anywhere to document the phases of excavation with photographs. These, along with his notes and drawings, were published in 1953 in three huge tomes that serve to this day as a point of reference for archaeological pursuits in the city.

Vittorio Spinazzola, second from the left in the photo above, hosts a dinner in the summer dining room of the House of the Moralist. Admonitory inscriptions adorn the walls of the room, which features its original table setting (right).

Members of Italy's Fine Arts Commission inspect a cleared section of the Via dell'Abbondanza in 1910 (left). *An ancient inscription can be seen on a wall on the left.*

of a united Italy under King Victor Emmanuel II in 1860. Keenly conscious of how the world valued his country's magnificent cultural heritage, Victor Emmanuel provided funds for a small army of workers at Pompeii, Herculaneum, and other sites in the vicinity. But his greatest contribution was the appointment of a man named Giuseppe Fiorelli as director of the excavations. A skilled archaeologist and the author of a history of Pompeii, Fiorelli would remain in charge until 1875.

His approach was the essence of discipline and orderliness. Beginning at Pompeii, he removed all the debris piled up during earlier excavations and then installed a drainage system to draw off rainwater that was tending to hasten decay at the site. After tracing the perimeter walls, he provided a map for the project by dividing the site into districts, or *regiones,* identifying individual blocks and carefully numbering buildings in a logical sequence. As the work proceeded, he made sure that every new object that emerged was given a precise description—not just of its appearance and nature, but also of its position and relationship to other objects. Whenever possible, new discoveries were left in place rather than removed for shipment to a museum or storehouse.

Bit by bit, as details accumulated and were pieced together by analytical methods, the long-buried past came alive. Because the cities and villas had been taken from the world almost intact, they could be brought back almost whole. Fiorelli demonstrated the possibilities, and many other gifted archaeologists have followed his lead. The result is an extraordinary drama, made all the more authentic by its mixing of the mundane and the apocalyptic.

In Pompeii, eggs and fish were found lying on a dining table; pots still contained meat bones, and shops still displayed, in desiccated form, onions, beans, olives, and figs. All manner of household effects remained in the rooms where they were used. Personal items of every kind turned up—jewelry, cosmetics, perfume, bronze mirrors, ivory combs, good-luck amulets. Herculaneum told the same story of ordinary life stopped in its tracks. Bread, salad, cakes, and fruit were found on one table; nuts were scattered on the counter of a shop; ropes and fishermen's

This wall painting—preserved by the ash that fell over Pompeii, and excavated along with many others like it—provides a glimpse of everyday life. Its kitchen motif includes pewter vessels, thrushes ready for the stewpot, an amphora casually leaning against the table, and a dish of eggs eerily similar to a real one uncovered intact from the ruins (inset).

nets were preserved; straw lay where it had just been removed from the packing case of a shipment of glassware.

After a fashion, voices could be heard as well. The walls of Pompeii were covered with graffiti—messages from lovers ("Successus the cloth-weaver loves Iris, the innkeeper's slave girl"), personal attacks ("Samius to Cornelius: Go hang yourself"), casual philosophizing ("No one is a gentleman who has not loved a woman"), and many more, of both general and specific application.

And then there were the people, recovered by a method that still seems almost magical.

Not long after he accepted his appointment, Fiorelli began thinking about the volcanic ash, picturing it drifting down from the sky, shaping itself to the contours of everything it touched. It would have seeped into the hair of victims, sifted into the folds of their garments, built up around arms that held the bodies of children, traced mouths frozen in a last gasp for air, modeled fingers curled in agony. He knew already from his digging that the once-powdery ash, having been moistened by rains after the eruption, had subsequently dried and hardened. This line of thinking suggested an intriguing possibility to him.

A colleague of Fiorelli's who visited Pompeii in 1863 reported that the moment of discovery occurred in February of that year, when a workman accidentally made a hole in a mound at the site with a careless swing of his pickax. "Signor Fiorelli perceived that there existed a cavity of some extent. He had for some time entertained the idea that there were probably human bodies buried in the ruins of the city, the remains of which might have perished, though leaving their impressions in the sandy covering. He therefore caused plaster of Paris in a very liquid state to be poured into the cavity." After the liquid plaster had had time to solidify, the cocoon of ash was removed, revealing a figure that was uncannily lifelike.

As more and more victims were recovered by this technique, fascination with the intimate details of Pompeii's tragic story grew. The casts fixed the terror and desperation of that long-ago disaster in a kind of eternal present: A woman holds an infant in her arms while two girls cling to the hem of her garment; a young man and woman fall side by side as they attempt to flee; outside the city's northern wall, a man collapses as he tries to pull his goat along by its halter.

Moments of collective death turned up everywhere. In a

house that belonged to a man named Quintus Poppaeus, 10 slaves succumbed on their way to an upstairs room; their leader held a bronze lantern. In the house of Publius Paquius Proculus, seven children were crushed when the second story gave way under the weight of pumice. In a building devoted to the wine trade, 34 people took refuge in a vault, bringing along bread and fruit to sustain them until the eruption had run its course; they never emerged. At a villa outside the city, 18 adults and 2 children died in the cellar; the master of the house, holding a silver key, died outside near a garden door leading to the fields, along with a steward who was carrying money and other valuables.

Many people were trying to save some of their belongings when they expired in the ash cloud. The mistress of one mansion expired outside her house in the company of three maids; around the bodies were strewn jewelry and money. Near the gladiators' barracks, a slave fell beside a horse that had been loaded with clothing and other useful articles.

From the first cast created by Giuseppe Fiorelli to the nine added in the summer of 1991, these frozen images of death deliver a shock, a jolt across the centuries. No one who views them can fail to sense the anguish of that time. The archaeologist who chronicled Fiorelli's discovery in 1863 said it as well as anyone when he described a cast of an adult male: One hand "is extended and strongly clenched, and the limbs in an attitude of rigidity almost amounting to convulsion. These facts, as well as the expression of pain and horror distinctly traceable in the countenance, would seem to show that the unfortunate man died fully conscious of the dreadful fate which awaited him, and against which he vainly struggled." Life's worst moment had arrived. He could not breathe.

THE HOUR OF DEATH

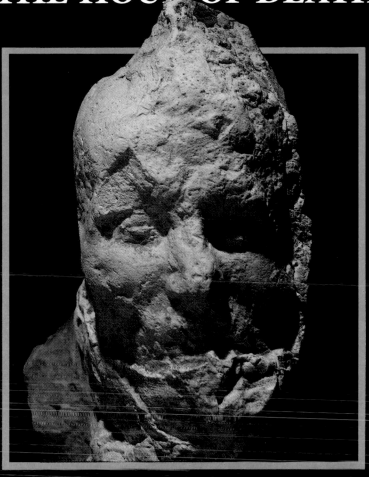

Among the myriad episodes of horror played out in Pompeii's final moments, the most poignant may well have been the last. One man, hoping to save both himself and his beloved dog, took shelter in a residence at the city's northern wall as Vesuvius wreaked its havoc. But when the danger apparently had passed, they found themselves sealed within the building by the ashfall: Their refuge had become a prison. In time, they met a grisly fate. The man slowly succumbed to starvation, and his faithful pet, mad with hunger, stripped the flesh from his bones.

The ordeal was a rare exception. Scores of victims perished instantly, struck down by the initial hail of glowing volcanic pumice. Hundreds more struggled above the rising tide of stony fragments only to be smothered in a cloud of poisonous gas and choking ash, their remains buried deep as still more debris rained down upon the city.

The very forces that doomed the citizens of Pompeii have conferred on them a kind of immortality. Skeletons are all that remain of those engulfed by the first fall of pumice or trapped in air pockets, such as the man and his dog. But the fine-grained ash accomplished a far more astounding preservation. Eventually hardening, it encased its victims and recorded the minutest details of their shapes long after their bodies had decayed. By filling the cavities with various compounds and then chipping away the surrounding shell, archaeologists have been able to create a virtual gallery of the dead.

The effect is staggering. Some victims show signs of struggling against their fate, while others appear resigned, almost peaceful. Many, like the figure above, tried to save themselves by breathing through a fold of cloth. One man, a watchman, quietly died at his station, steadfastly refusing to abandon his post. Whatever the pose, these visions of the dead remain indelible nearly 2,000 years later, their hands in many cases reaching out across the centuries as if in supplication.

The first wave of coarse volcanic fall-out to reach Pompeii felled hundreds, collapsing roofs and crushing those huddled inside. Near the spot where this skeleton lies, a prophetic line of poetry was found scratched onto a wall: "Nothing in the world," it read, "can endure forever."

Held fast by his collar and chain, this dog could not escape as a shower of rock poured through the open ceiling of an atrium like the sand in an inverted hourglass. As the hot pumice piled up, the dog climbed as high as he could. When the chain would reach no farther, the cloud of ash encased him.

As the rising level of rocky debris threatened to overwhelm him, this man sought safety in the branches of a tall tree. The strategy was doomed to failure; within moments, the poison cloud enveloped him. The limb of the tree, which broke under his weight, is still clutched firmly between his legs.

An aged beggar, found with the sack that he used to collect alms, collapsed as he fled toward the sea through the city's southern gate. On his feet were an incongruously handsome pair of sandals—a gift from public charity or, perhaps, a last-minute acquisition.

An adult man (above) and a young
child (below) look deceptively peaceful
in death, as if they had merely slipped
into their final sleep. Their positions,
their facial expressions, even the folds
of their clothing remain plainly visible after more than 19 centuries.

A servant, heavily laden with a bag full of provisions, died as he led two small boys and their mother through a blinding swirl of black smoke across a perilous mire of gravel. A piece of tile and an iron utensil were discovered nearby, probably used by the boys to ward off falling debris.

Straining to reach his fallen wife and child, a man managed to rise to a crouch before he, too, was overcome by lethal fumes. "And all was consumed in the flames, all covered with the gray ash," lamented the Roman poet Martial, "and the gods themselves would that they had not such power."

ACROSS THE AGES, THE HUM OF LIFE

*Lines of graceful
pillars mark the
remains of Pom-
peii's gladiator
barracks, home to
some of the city's
most public heroes.
Found in the ruins
were the ornate
bronze helmet at
top left and the
handsome leg
guard, or greave,
at bottom right.*

Almost a century before Giuseppe Fiorelli's amazing casts of Vesuvius' victims stirred broad interest in the human side of Pompeii's story, a discovery of skeletal remains at one particular spot piqued the curiosity of even the most plunder-minded excavators of the day. The find came to light during a prolonged period of exploratory digging in the winter of 1767-68 as workers cleared debris from a building that had served as a barracks for gladiators— trained fighters who provided brutal entertainment for the populace by battling each other and wild animals in Pompeii's Amphitheater. Some of them had chosen their profession as a way to climb out of poverty; others were prisoners of war, slaves, or debtors; and a few were condemned criminals.

These were tough men, thoroughly schooled in the art of killing, hardened by the knowledge that they might end their days in the arena, sprawled in agony on the blood-soaked earth as thousands of spectators howled in delight. For many of them, however, death had come in a totally unexpected fashion, and had not even given them a fighting chance.

As the diggers made their way around the southeast corner of the barracks and headed up its long eastern side, they came upon dozens of skeletons—more than 50 by the final tally. Among those caught by the catastrophe were two wretches still bound by chains to the barracks walls. But someone from a very different stratum of society was here as well—a woman of wealth and style, her bones still bedecked with pearls, rings, and other expensive jewelry.

Was she a rich sponsor of a group of fighters, felled during a routine inspection of her charges? Or had she been making a special visit to a favored champion on that fateful night? A romantic encounter could not be ruled out, especially after later excavations revealed graffiti attesting to female admiration of successful gladiators: "Caladus, the Thracian, makes all the girls sigh," read one of these wall scribblings; "Crescens, the net fighter, holds the hearts of all the girls," noted another. But scholarly opinion eventually came to favor a less titillating explanation of the woman's presence. The barracks stood near a gate leading out of the city and down to the Sarno River. As Vesuvius flamed and belched through the night of August 24, many people gathered in this area, huddling under any available roof, ready to flee toward the water if the eruption did not abate. Most likely, the elegantly attired woman was simply part of this throng.

No matter why she was there, the find is yet another example of the time-stopping uniqueness of Pompeii, preserving as in a snapshot the details of a desperately confused moment from long ago. And although those who unearthed this intriguing evidence soon turned back to the greedy search for material trophies, the discovery was a harbinger of the archaeological future. Beginning in the 19th

The map below shows Pompeii's outer walls and the excavated portions of the city, including the rectangular residential blocks separated by narrow streets and the wide main thoroughfares that created a gridlike pattern emulating Greek city plans. Thirty-five of the more important buildings and sites are numbered on the map and identified below.

1 HOUSE OF L. CAECILIUS JUCUNDUS
2 HOUSE OF THE MORALIST
3 HOUSE OF JULIA FELIX
4 HOUSE OF THE VETTII
5 HOUSE OF THE SILVER WEDDING
6 HOUSE OF THE FAUN
7 HOUSE OF MENANDER
8 HOUSE OF OCTAVIUS QUARTO
9 HOUSE OF THE SURGEON
10 HOUSE OF THE ANCIENT HUNT
11 HOUSE OF L. CEIUS SECUNDUS
12 VILLA OF CICERO

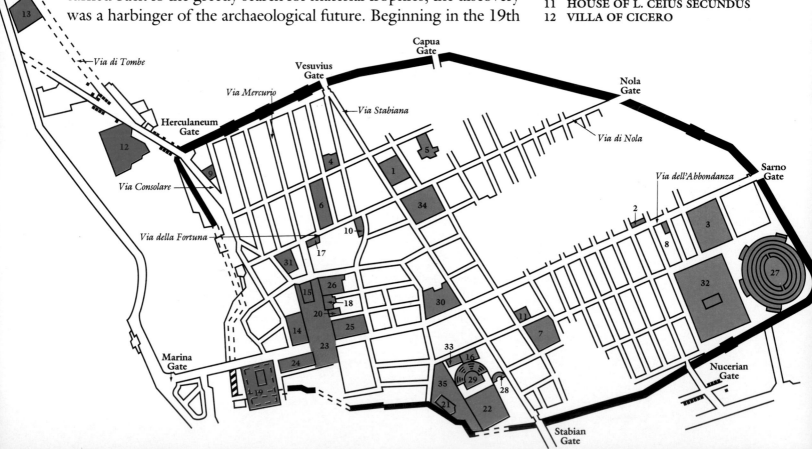

century and continuing to the present day, investigators would focus on Pompeii as a living community rather than a trove of statuary and mosaics. Whole careers would be devoted to determining how Pompeians earned their livelihood, governed their city, worshiped their gods, socialized, amused themselves, and carried out the full gamut of daily activities, from shopping to bathing. Archaeologists would perform near miracles in restitching the fabric of the community—the streets, markets, theaters, temples, and taverns that were the essence of Roman city life. Bit by bit, they would assemble a remarkably detailed image of Pompeii in its prime—a picture that would greatly deepen scholars' understanding of the classical world.

Fiorelli was, of course, the prime mover in preserving this ancient metropolis as it was. Without his efforts, the city might very well have been stripped of all its riches, the glorious immediacy of its shops and homes and thoroughfares destroyed forever. To a large extent, he also set the stage for those who succeeded him. One of the first of these was a German archaeologist named August Mau, who did as much as anyone to breathe life into the civic bones of Pompeii and give it back its history.

Working at the site throughout the last quarter of the 19th century, Mau examined construction materials and pored over ornamental details of the buildings to identify major architectural styles associated with specific historical periods. His study of the use of a type of volcanic rock called gray tufa, for example, showed that the stone predominated in structures erected during the second century BC. With the aid of Mau's stylistic categories, other researchers developed systems of dating that revealed how Pompeii had grown and changed over the course of its centuries-long history. In addition, Mau drafted plans of virtually every major edifice in the city, and elaborated on Fiorelli's street map. Among his most scholarly contributions was a study of the subject matter of Pompeii's colorful wall paintings.

Mau published prolifically on all aspects of the ruins, issuing his results in bulletins printed by his sponsor, the German Archaeological Institute. *Pompeii, Its Life and Art*—his revision of an earlier work by J. A. Overbeck—is one of the liveliest volumes on the subject and remains in print almost a century later. Much to his disappointment, these exhaustive labors did not win Mau adequate recognition from his employers, who passed him over for top appointments. But his accomplishments were undeniable. As well as providing an understanding of how the community had evolved from the time of its founding, he was the first to draw a convincing portrait of Pompeii on the eve of Vesuvius' eruption.

As the depths of its history were illuminated by Mau and others, and the texture of Pompeii's everyday life grew clearer, the ghostly city began to reawaken in people's imaginations: The pumping of its economic heart could be sensed among the stones; a Mediterranean sensuality could be read in the ruins; Pompeii assumed a personality—vivid, voluble, sometimes violent.

Pompeii under the Romans was conspicuously prosperous, a city blessed by nature and well served by its inhabitants. All through the year, boats could be seen bringing cargoes up the Sarno River and carrying goods away to the wider world. Maritime trade lent Pompeii a cosmopolitan flavor, but most of its wealth derived from agriculture. In the fields outside the city, large flocks of sheep supported a thriving wool industry. Neat ranks of grapevines running up the slopes of Vesuvius to the north produced the region's famed sweet wine. Higher still, villa owners cultivated olives; some were sold for eating, but much of the harvest was converted into oil, as is indicated by the fact that presses have been found both on farms and in the town itself.

Roman engineering had put its stamp on this pastoral landscape. Across the fields ran an arched stone aqueduct, which began at springs in the mountains 25 miles to the east and split into two branches, one heading northwest to Neapolis and the other entering Pompeii from the north. The aqueduct supplied the city with much of the water for its numerous street-side fountains, as well as for the *thermae,* or hot baths, that were so integral to Roman social life. Wells dug within Pompeii in pre-Roman times had previously been the main source of water, and these had remained in use during the days of empire, complementing the aqueduct. More than a dozen water towers scattered around the city served as reservoirs for the aqueduct. Pressure created by the long downhill flow from the mountains forced water up lead pipes into tanks at the

GRAFFITI: THE PEOPLE SPEAK

"Romula tarried here with Staphylus." "O Chius, I hope that your ulcerous pustules reopen and burn even more than they did before." "Vote for Lucius Popidius Sabinus. His grandmother worked hard for his last election and is pleased with the results." "Health to those who invite me to lunch."

Such graffiti and thousands more in mad variety have been found throughout Pompeii by archaeologists. Scribbling for popular consumption was apparently vital to the commonweal. Of 6,000 public inscriptions uncovered in the city, fully one-half were graffiti, personal messages that ranged from emotional pleas or curses to lyrical encomiums. Indeed, there were so many messages that one *scriptor* wrote, "I am surprised, O wall, that you, who have to bear the weariness of so many writers, are still standing."

Graffiti derives from an Italian

verb meaning "to scratch," and that is how the Pompeians etched their messages on whitewashed plaster walls. They used a stylus or even a nail or piece of wood. The most common graffiti were purely personal—slaves complaining about their masters or lotharios offering erotic commentary. A high degree of literacy and humor went hand in hand with gleeful vulgarity. When a suspicious swain writes, "No more question of it—Romula, my mistress, has slept here with her lover," the reader can almost hear the sigh behind his reluctant conclusion. Thus, in quotidian, unpretentious messages do the very walls of Pompeii tell of the lively people who built them.

Unlike most graffiti, which were scratched into public walls, this formal message—only partly visible—was daubed in red pigment like that found in the clay bowl inset below right. Other, less formal signs warned people against vandalizing individual houses or using the streets as lavatories.

top of the towers, most of which were nearly 20 feet tall; the drop from there through a series of smaller pipes made fountains gush throughout the city. Mau was so impressed with the whole system that he assumed everyone must have had plenty of running water readily available. In fact, the quantity could be limited, and most families—even the wealthier ones—had to rely on the dozens of public fountains for much of their freshwater supplies. In addition, cement-lined cisterns, some under the portico floors of public buildings, stored rainwater channeled from roofs; private homes also had pools for collecting rain.

The most common approach to the city was from the northwest—that is, from Neapolis and Rome. From this direction, Pompeii conveyed the impression of a well-fortified town: Two monumental portals, the Herculaneum and Vesuvius gates, offered entrance through the city wall—more than 30 feet high in places—and a trio of square towers loomed between them. Elsewhere around the city, 10 other strategically placed towers stood atop the ramparts. The wall itself was constructed of earth and rubble and faced with rough-hewn blocks of limestone and volcanic rock. These perimeter defenses, probably built in the third century BC, had at one time entirely enclosed Pompeii's 160 gently sloping acres. Except between the two northwest gates, the wall's masons had followed the course of a natural scarp, a steep drop-off created far back in geologic time when a thick tongue of molten lava creeping down from the volcano's summit had hardened in its tracks.

Six other gates ringed the city, including the narrow, south-facing Stabian—the oldest entrance—which fronted on an ancient moat, and the barrel-vaulted Marina Gate, granting access from the Sarno River up a steep ramp and stairway. The gates were swung shut every evening and reopened in the morning, events that in latter days had become little more than ritual gestures, setting the tempo of the Pompeian day. But earlier in the city's history, such precautions had been well founded, and at various times the wall and its fortified portals had protected the inhabitants from attack. Signs of damage inflicted during the siege by the Roman general Sulla in 89 BC can still be seen on the wall's facing stones, particularly near the Vesuvius Gate. Once Rome had gained unchallenged authority throughout the Italian Peninsula, the battlements ceased to serve a military function, and as Pompeii became an increasingly popular spot for retired military people and

The rough, wheel-rutted cobbles of the wide Via della Fortuna are punctuated by sidewalk-level steppingstones that kept the feet of crossing pedestrians out of the street's damp and muck. At right are the ruins of the Temple of Fortuna Augusta, the large sanctuary that gave the street its name.

wealthy Romans, some sections of the wall were actually torn down to make way for expansion.

Archaeologists, of course, centered their attention on the many buildings and monuments that lay within these ramparts. As they uncovered the city, the job of identification was greatly eased by inscriptions—ready-made labels, in effect. As was common throughout the Roman world, such commemorations were often quite verbose, recording the name, use, date of construction, and sponsorship of a structure. Even renovations to existing buildings might sport lengthy explanations. When a wall was added to close off a colonnaded passageway beside the Temple of Apollo—an action that blocked the view from the windows of adjacent houses—an inscription was appended that not only named the two minor elected magistrates involved, but also set out the 3,000 sesterces fee decreed by the city council that gave them the right "to shut off light" and build "to the height of the tiles"—that is, to the level of the rooftops.

To a newcomer, Pompeii's layout—affected as it was by the city's long history—could be confusing. As Fiorelli discovered in the 1860s, an irregular network of streets dominated the oldest precincts, in the southwest corner. Archaeologists have established that the Samnites engineered these areas in the fourth century BC, after subduing the native Oscans. Restricted by the natural contours of the volcanic terrain, the Samnites built a triangular forum and warren of crooked thoroughfares. Subsequent expansion of the city followed the standard Hellenistic pattern, a strict grid of elongated blocks known by the Romans as *insulae,* or islands.

Throughout the city, less traveled streets spanned no more than about 15 feet, sidewalks included. Narrow byways were a clever adaptation to the intense Mediterranean sun: The sidewalks and road surfaces, carefully paved with cut blocks of basalt lava, were generally bathed in shadow, which kept things relatively cool. Sea breezes, which began blowing around 10 o'clock in the morning and continued until late afternoon, provided further relief.

Five or six main routes crisscrossed the city. Traffic entering from the northwest flowed along two wide, angling streets, the Via Consolare or the Via Stabiana. The first led, with a few sharp turns, from the Herculaneum Gate to the Temple of Jupiter, at the north end of the town's main forum; the second, starting at the Vesuvius Gate, bisected the city from northwest to southeast, exiting to the south at the low-lying Stabian Gate. Close to 26 feet wide along most

of its length, the Via Stabiana was a principal thoroughfare, accommodating overland trade with cities to the north and almost constantly noisy with the rumble of carts. Vehicles traveling southbound would cross, at roughly equal intervals, the Via di Nola and the Via dell'Abbondanza—"street of abundance"—both also about 26 feet wide. (Many of these names, bestowed by archaeologists, refer either to communities beyond the walls to which the roads led or to a noteworthy feature; the Via dell'Abbondanza, for example, was lined with a number of shops.) Centuries of hard use had worn ruts as much as 10 inches deep in the paving stones of these broad boulevards. In other areas of the city, vehicular traffic was restricted; many side streets were for pedestrians only.

Early in the 20th century, Vittorio Spinazzola, the most energetic director of excavations at Pompeii since Fiorelli, oversaw an ambitious project to reconstruct the Via dell'Abbondanza, which had been subject to fitful excavation since the 1830s. With the flare of a showman, he viewed the digs, in the words of one commentator, as "archaeological theater." Like August Mau, he considered his profession not a dull, scholarly pursuit, but rather a chance to re-create an ancient ambience. Beginning work on the Via dell'Abbondanza in 1910, he kept at the task for the next 13 years. So monumental was the labor that another 12 years would pass before his successor, Amedeo Maiuri, finished the job in 1935.

Archaeologists had traditionally worked down through ruins, removing successive layers of debris to proceed further back in time. Spinazzola showed that it was also possible to work up. Describing

In an antique version of a steam table, earthenware jars that held warm food and drink sit in the counters of a thermopolium (far left), a small fast-food spot on the busy Via dell'Abbondanza. At near left stands a bronze scale with Mercury's head used as a counterweight.

Four round mills for grinding grain into flour stand near the brick oven in the bakery of Modestus, one of many such establishments in Pompeii. Eightyone loaves of bread like the one shown directly below were found in the oven.

his methods in three lavishly illustrated volumes, he explained how fragments of tile roofs, walls, and balconies that had originally formed the second story of a building could be identified and fitted together to reconstruct the complete facade as it had stood before being toppled in the eruption. Crew members kept a full photographic record of the process and were taught the fine points of ancient construction techniques so that they could comprehend, when looking at a jumble of debris, how to reassemble the puzzle. Gradually, the Via dell'Abbondanza came together in all its variety— a mix of private homes, taverns, bakeries, groceries, workshops, and other enterprises. Along the reconstituted urban artery, the sights, sounds, and smells of another age were almost palpable.

One can imagine people strolling down this quintessential Main Street in all kinds of weather. They could find shelter from sudden downpours simply by stepping under handy balconies, overhangs, or porticoes, several of which were reconstructed by Spinazzola. Because of Pompeii's general lack of storm drains, streams of runoff after heavy rains turned the roadway into a small river, but raised sidewalks kept pedestrians' feet dry and prevented shop floors from getting soaked. They were useful even on dry days, since wastewater and garbage in ill-defined gutters were a constant nuisance. Those wishing to cross usually did so at a corner, using large steppingstones that were placed at sidewalk level. The stones were arranged so that the gaps between them allowed carriage and cart wheels to roll past unimpeded.

Shops along the Via dell'Abbondanza and other streets were often part of a house and were either rented out or run by the owner. Although many establishments were relatively spacious, some were mere alcoves, 8 by 10 feet or less; they could be closed at night behind wooden shutters. A typical one might consist of no more than a wide counter across the front, frequently veneered with marble, with insets for terra-cotta vessels; snack bars would specialize in two or three items—wine, meats, goat cheese, or dry goods such as lentils or nuts. Poorer Pompeians, who often lacked cooking facilities, might take their meals at these neighborhood stands. One on the Via dell'Abbondanza may have prepared hearty bean and lentil stews: Deep earthenware jars found at the site could have been used to store such concoctions.

Workshops were less common, but here and there in the city diggers have come upon signs of glassblowers, bronze workers, blacksmiths, and artisans specializing in silver and gold. A pottery just outside the Herculaneum Gate was equipped with two kilns for firing finished pieces, and an assortment of vessels have been uncovered, including pitchers in the shape of roosters and fish. One shop off the Via dell'Abbondanza sold iron tools, and archaeologists have determined that most common utensils were locally crafted. Nevertheless, many items appear to have been imports: Some pots, pans, and other household accouterments came from Spain, Asia Minor, and the Aegean world.

Throughout the city, *pistrinae,* or bakeries, abounded. Pompeii had at least 30 commercial bakeries, 20 of which had their own mills and masonry ovens. Donkeys and slave labor were used to turn the hourglass-shaped mills and grind flour daily. (The Roman statesman Cato, known for his thriftiness, recommended Pompeii as a good place to buy a millstone—undoubtedly because volcanic rock, an excellent material for the purpose, was so plentiful there.) Bakers patted most loaves into flattened rounds indented so that they would break into eight pie-shaped wedges. But excavators have also found molds that would have sculpted dough into exotic griffin heads and

Whimsical wall paintings from the House of the Vettii portray cupids working at Pompeian trades. At top the cupids make olive oil, a pair of them working the press (far right) *while others at center heat and stir the oil in kettles and those at far left store and sell the finished product. In the lower panel, cupids act as goldsmiths. A pair* (right) *tend a furnace, two more use an anvil* (left), *another hammers on a nearly completed bowl, and a salescupid at near left weighs an ornament on a hand scale.*

other shapes, and one bakery even sold its own brand of dog biscuit. In another shop, an inscription on the wall listed goods and prices, given in terms of the *as,* a coin worth about a penny. This particular establishment did not confine its merchandise to baked products, selling also oil, hay, bran, and flowery wreaths that might be worn as necklaces on some of the many ceremonial occasions that crowded the Roman calendar.

At its western end, the Via dell'Abbondanza emptied into the main forum, a rectangular space measuring almost 500 feet long by more than 150 feet wide that functioned as the heart of the city and was the scene of a weekly market, among other things. An ancient site dating back to Pompeii's earliest days, it was replanned and formalized toward the close of the second century BC. All but foot traffic was barred by three large upright stones placed across the entrance at the Via dell'Abbondanza.

As was the case everywhere in the Mediterranean world, the Forum operated as a kind of magnet, pulling citizens toward it. It was the spot for dickering over purchases, for carrying out municipal business, for catching up on the latest news and gossip, for people watching, for attending religious services, for seeing the sights. A pleasant hubbub would issue from the shifting crowds strolling across the limestone pavement, hurrying to a nearby government building on some important errand, or gathering beside the large columns of the double-tiered, two-story colonnade around the perimeter. On some days, the noise level would rise to a sustained din of political debates, celebratory processions, musical performances, and vendors hawking their wares—a swirling social drama eminently suited to Pompeian tastes. But there was always an aura of dignity as well: All around the Forum were statues, at least 40 of them, installed to honor the gods, emperors, generals, and other architects of Roman greatness. The emperor Augustus himself had decreed that important public places should have such inspirational decoration; his own likeness was to be included, of course, along with those of prominent forebears stretching back to the mythical Aeneas.

The buildings flanking the Forum encompassed a number of distinctive styles, executed in a range of different materials. Mau established that the oldest structures—dating from before the third century BC—were crafted from a porous, yellowish limestone, also found in many houses of approximately the same period throughout the city. Later masons working in the area of the Forum employed

FOR A PLEASURE-LOVING PUBLIC, A WEALTH OF THEATRICAL SPECTACLES

Next to violent gladiatorial combat, the citizens of Pompeii seem most to have enjoyed flocking to the theater to attend plays and other entertainments. They had plenty of chances to do so. The larger of the city's two theaters, with seats for 5,000 spectators, could hold no less than one-fourth of the entire population. Even the smaller theater accommodated an audience of 1,200.

And besides plays, there were performances to mark the city's many religious festivals—at least 60 of them a year.

The larger theater was magnificent, proof in itself of the Pompeians' passion for drama. Built between 200-150 BC, more than a century before the first permanent theater in Rome, it was copied in part from the lovely theaters of ancient Greece,

with its symmetrical horseshoe of serried stone seats snugly embedded in a natural hillside. A large stage at the rear provided the setting for colorful backdrops. The theater also boasted a vast awning that, stretched on poles, shielded the spectators from the summer sun—not to mention a wonderful device that showered them between acts with cooling sprays of water.

Contrasting with the grotesque comic mask at top, the mosaic at left shows the sort of stylized mask with gaping mouth and ornate hairdo worn by actors playing parts in tragedies.

Pompeii's compact theater district appears vividly in an aerial photograph, the large theater with its semicircle of seats and wide stage at left, its smaller neighbor at top right. Known as an odeon, the small one was originally covered by a wooden roof and was used for the more intimate forms of entertainment such as concerts, readings, and orations.

A stage set in Pompeii's theater may well have looked like this one in a mural from Herculaneum. Here, the stage's rear wall was made to look like the front of an ornate palace.

The spectacles given in Pompeii's large theater must have been wildly varied. Some days there were Greek tragedies. More popular were comedies by Roman authors such as Plautus that mocked the ways of misers, knavish slaves, and strutting, oafish generals. There were pantomimes as well, balletlike performances by actors who were so skilled they could by gesture alone portray every emotion from horror to joy. Most popular of all were farces in which the comedians racketed about the stage playing gluttons and buffoons, penny pinchers, and thieves.

Loving the theater, the Pompeians plastered the city's walls with graffiti praising their favorite players. Best loved was a pantomimist called Paris whose name appears over and over. "Paris, the sweet darling," sighs one message, while other tributes are signed adoringly, "The Comrades of Paris Club."

In the mosaic above, actors rehearse a satyr play, an early form of theater borrowed from Greece. The men at left practice dance steps while a musician plays a double pipe.

In a wall painting, a handsome actor rests after a performance. He probably played a king in a tragedy since he holds a scepter and has a purple mantle across his lap, and a tragic mask can be seen resting on a table near a box of costumes.

A mask denoting a courtesan hides the identity of a player molded in terra cotta (right), who may well have been a male, in keeping with an old theatrical convention. At left is the bust of Caius Norbanus Serix, an actor so admired he was elected magistrate of a Pompeian suburb.

C NORBANI
SORICIS
SECVNDARVM
MAG PACI
AVG FELICIS
SVBVRBANI
EX D D
LOC D

59

volcanic tufa, which was relatively lightweight and easy to cut. White Carrara marble and assorted colored marbles were also common in the Forum. In addition, brick, wood, terra cotta, white limestone, and stucco have been found.

Contrary to popular notions, many of the bare white stucco and marble surfaces visible today were originally painted. Styles and tastes varied over the four centuries of construction for which archaeologists have found evidence, but in the period just preceding the volcano's eruption, the preference was for the most vivid hues. Many of the buildings around the Forum were bedecked in bright reds, yellows, and greens, with contrasting touches of black. Columns and friezes were frequent objects of such decoration.

Places of worship were integral elements in the Forum complex. When the Forum was first laid out, its designers used one side of the Temple of Apollo for its western boundary. Across the shorter northern side arose an imposing temple dedicated to Jupiter, king of the gods. Along with virtually every other major building, the Temple of Jupiter sustained considerable damage in the earthquake that rocked the area in AD 62. Although the Pompeians soon began work on repairs, many structures around the Forum were still under renovation at the time of the Vesuvian eruption. The Temple of Jupiter had actually been turned into a workshop, with uncut blocks of basalt, stonecutting tools, and other building supplies stored there. In the 19th century, diggers even came upon an example of sculptural recycling in the making: Some thrifty artist had selected the torso of a colossal stone statue and was carving it into a smaller figure.

If the Forum served as a religious center, it also held the city's key secular monuments. Most impressive was the huge Basilica, built just south of the Temple of Apollo at about the same time as the Temple of Jupiter. This was the main stamping ground of the city's movers and shakers. Conversing in the aisles of the vast main hall, which was supported by 28 gigantic columns with brick shafts, they greased the day-to-day machinery of Pompeii. In and out of the spacious edifice bustled magistrates, perhaps on their way from the adjoining municipal buildings to the Basilica's tribunal room, where they tried civil cases.

Many of the details of local rule are amply described in Roman texts. Pompeii had four magistrates, all elected annually. Two bore

Open to the sun like a piazza in a modern Italian city, Pompeii's long rectangular Forum, marked by the remains of its great colonnade, lies amid the ruins of temples, markets, and other large buildings. At upper right stand the remains of the city's great Temple of Jupiter; at the opposite end of the Forum are the walls of three similarly shaped buildings that probably housed municipal offices. To the bottom left of the Forum is the Basilica, an ancestor of the modern court of law, outlined by its own rows of columns, while to the right of the Forum is the outline of the clothmakers' large guildhall, the Building of Eumachia.

the title *duumvir*—the term means "one man of two"—and were charged with numerous supervisory functions, including presiding over the city's legislative assemblies. The other two, called aediles, tended to assorted administrative matters, among them maintaining public buildings, streets, and water supplies. Marketers hoping to open new businesses, promoters wishing to stage gladiatorial games, and laborers wanting municipal jobs such as street cleaning all sought out these officials, who would dispense the appropriate licenses. Pompeii also had a city council, whose 80 to 100 members served for life. Some investigators have speculated that they met in one of a trio of halls at the Forum's south end.

In addition to all its other functions, the Forum served as a kind of clearinghouse for official notices. At one end stood a wall dedicated to disseminating such information as police regulations or court sentences. Specialists known as *dealbatores,* or whitewashers, were hired to periodically paint over the wall to provide a clean surface; afterward, *scriptores,* or sign painters, would amend and update the notices, using red or black paint. During elections, this wall and others all over the city were filled with the Pompeian version of campaign posters. In Pompeii's final days, some 1,500 such inscriptions were vying for public attention in anticipation of an upcoming vote.

On the Forum's east side, a particularly grand edifice proclaimed the importance of the fullery business—the cleansing, scouring, thickening, and dyeing of woolen cloth. Its construction had been funded by a woman named Eumachia, widow of a cloth dealer; an inscription indicated that she had done so "in her own name and that of her son," who was doubtless too young at the time to take on the responsibility. Headquarters for the fullers' guild, the imposing, wide-porticoed Building of Eumachia also served as warehouse and showroom for the members' goods, both raw wool and woven cloth.

By the first century AD, the power of the fullers was everywhere visible in Pompeii. Excavators have identified 39 separate sites where they plied their craft; a number of these structures were the former homes of well-to-do Pompeians who

A REFINED BUT RISKY ART

Medicine—or at least surgery—was surprisingly advanced in Pompeii, as is shown by the painting below and the instruments at bottom right. In the painting, a kneeling surgeon uses forceps to carefully remove an arrowhead from the thigh of Aeneas, hero of the poet Virgil's epic, the *Aeneid,* while a sympathetic goddess and a weeping boy look on.

These surgical instruments are a small sampling of the large number of items, ranging from delicate probes and scalpels to fine-tooth saws and clamps, found in Pompeii. One building contained so many instruments that archaeologists dubbed it (naturally enough)

the House of the Surgeon.

But if Roman doctors—who most often were slaves or freedmen—were skilled at surgery, their other medical practices seem dubious. There were no anesthetics or antiseptics, and while some physicians employed herbs such as rosemary and sage that did have some curative powers, they also prescribed such strange nostrums as lizard dung, pigeon blood, earthworm ash, and fox liver. It is little wonder that doctors were regarded with some skepticism by the people, who offered up prayers for recovery to the gods rather than to the medical profession.

The scalpel, scissors, speculum, and bone forceps shown below closely resemble modern surgical tools except for being made of bronze and iron rather than high-grade steel. Especially sophisticated was the speculum, which was used for gynecological examinations.

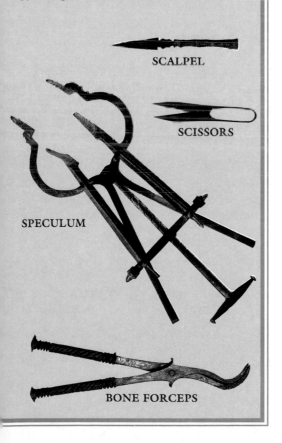

SCALPEL

SCISSORS

SPECULUM

BONE FORCEPS

may have moved to country villas after the earthquake. At 12 locations, new cloth—still greasy from the lanolin of the sheep—was prepared for garments. Wall paintings in a fullery on the Via Mercurio—running north from the Forum—outline some of the steps in the process. In one panel, workers stand in large vats, kneading cloth. As elsewhere in the empire, the Pompeians would have filled these vats with an astringent substance called fuller's earth, an absorbent clay that contained ash and urine. (Fullers also served as ancient versions of the dry cleaner, taking in soiled togas and other clothing and subjecting them to a similar regimen.) In another panel of the fullery paintings, a workman combs new cloth with a thin metal card to raise the nap. After these operations, the cloth would be spread on a special frame and bleached white by sulfur fumes.

At other shops around town, workers added dyes stored in clay amphorae to cauldrons of boiling water that had been filled with previously cleansed cloth; archaeologists have found intact containers of the pigments and have also unearthed lead kettles used for the boiling at several sites. Four shops in Pompeii made felt from wool scraps, and although most cloth was woven elsewhere in the region, the city did have six spinning and weaving establishments. Little wonder the fullers' umbrella organization commanded such an eminent spot on the Forum.

Just north of the Building of Eumachia was the city's primary market, the Macellum, a colonnaded court at the Forum's northeast corner. Painted scenes discovered in a private house in Pompeii portray this area as the ancient equivalent of a shopping mall. On the wall of a potter's shop on the Via dell'Abbondanza, a notice reads, "Markets are held in Pompeii and Nuceria on Saturdays, at Atella and Nola on Sundays." Every Saturday, then, in the colonnade beyond the Macellum's splendid facade of 16 white, statue-flanked marble columns, sellers set up booths where shoppers could purchase fresh fruits and vegetables, grains, spices, and prepared foods, all of which have been found in carbonized form at various excavation sites. At an airy, 12-sided pavilion in the open courtyard, salesmen plucked live fish from a tank and cleaned them for customers. (Excavators have come upon large piles of discarded scales in this area, indicating a lively trade.) From small tables, merchants hawked apples, pears, plums, figs, raisins, preserved fruits, and chestnuts. Some of the produce they sold was grown in garden plots within the city walls.

To ensure that vendors in the Forum gave fair weight of such items as lentils, hempseed, and other bulk goods, the city government operated an office for monitoring weights and measures near the Temple of Apollo. In a small alcove there, an official manned a limestone table containing bowl-shaped cavities, which were designed to hold dry or liquid substances in amounts precisely corresponding to the Roman standard. Plugs at their base allowed the cavities to be drained after the measurement had been made.

Busy as they were, Pompeians did not neglect their leisure. Archaeologists have calculated that about 10 percent of the excavated land within Pompeii's walls was given over to sports and entertainment facilities—an amphitheater, exercise grounds, public baths, and two theaters *(pages 56-59)*. In addition, the city had a multitude of taverns, inns, and brothels; these were concentrated in the older section of town and also near the city gates, perhaps as an enticement to out-of-town visitors. The largest hotel, less than two blocks off the Via dell'Abbondanza, had space for 50 guests—most of them no doubt government officials, traders, or tourists. Across the street, a much smaller inn served meals in a dining room fitted with three elegant couches. Two spacious hostelries near the Herculaneum Gate could accommodate chariots and wagons that pulled into large front driveways to discharge passengers. Better hotels such as the magnificent old House of Sallust (a converted dwelling) might also have garden restaurants where guests could dine under canopies of trees.

At some lodgings, rooms were set aside for drinking and dice playing. More frequently, however, men would indulge these pastimes in wineshops, small street-side bars, and *cauponae,* or taverns; all told, archaeologists have counted 138 of these various sorts of watering holes throughout the city. The taverns commonly occupied block corners and could be entered from two streets. Coming into the caupona of Euxinus, a fairly representative tavern located near the Amphitheater, a reveler would be greeted first by a painting of a phoenix and two peacocks, and a slogan reading, "You too will enjoy the Happy Phoenix." He could choose to eat at a counter in front, at a table in the large dining room at the rear, or in the garden.

Taverns offered fare typical of modern pubs. Simple meals of cheese, bread, sausages, and wine—either cold or mulled—made fine accompaniments to gambling games with dice or board games such as checkers. Patrons must have had their favorite hangouts, and a

A solid brick-and-stone building that housed a brothel operated—so inscriptions say—by two worthies named Victor and Africanus still stands at the corner of two Pompeian streets. At right a comparatively tame painting of brothel life shows a woman, seductively garbed in a transparent blouse, handing something, perhaps a payment, to a servant while her customer prepares to drain a drinking horn, or rhyton. A busy trading center, Pompeii had several brothels for the entertainment of traveling merchants.

tavernkeeper who offered poor value quickly became known. Outside one dive, a disgruntled customer had scrawled, "Would that you pay for all your tricks, innkeeper. You sell us water and keep the good wine for yourself."

Other cauponae sold sex as well. In one such establishment, an infamous madam named Asellina advertised the availability of both heated wine and prostitutes, who tended to their clients in small rooms adjoining the main one. The Taverna Lusoria provided credit and gambling—and, on the second floor, cubicles for dalliances. Typically, tavern walls were covered with erotic paintings and graffiti, as well as portraits of Priapus, the god of fecundity, endowed with an outsize phallus.

Just as some Pompeian men must have passed a good portion of their evenings at taverns, they spent most afternoons at the public baths. The Stabian, oldest of the baths, with facilities for both men and women, sat at the intersection of Stabiana and Abbondanza streets and appears to have been under repair when Vesuvius erupted: Archaeologists discovered entombed in the ash a construction crew that, at the time of the disaster, had been engaged in laying pipe. The Forum Baths near the city center included a garden. Although smaller than the Stabian, they made up for it with an interior filled with landscape paintings and elaborate stucco decorations. Excavators unearthed 1,328 oil lamps within the complex, indicating that the baths were open at night.

Unlike modern health clubs, the baths cultivated a relaxed atmosphere. Beginning at midday, Pompeians filtered in to bathe, swim, and exercise—or, in winter, to warm themselves up, since homes had only the most primitive heating systems. Although patrons would doubtless have their own specific routines, a sort of generic drill can be discerned. First, they undressed in an outer locker room and gave their clothes to a slave for safekeeping. Then they subjected themselves to a series of increasingly hotter soakings, moving from a *tepidarium,* or warm room, to a *caldarium,* or hot room, and perhaps on to a *laconicum,* or sauna. One particularly ingenious technique for heating the baths was devised early in the first century BC by a man named Gaius Sergius Orata, who initially earned his livelihood harvesting oysters. Aware that oysters grow more rapidly in warm water, he began raising them year round in tanks supported by brick pillars and heated from below by air circulated through furnaces. The method worked so well that Orata developed a version for human use, designing a system in which steam and water flowed from boilers through flues and pipes to heat rooms or baths. Behind the scenes, slaves stoked the flames of the furnaces, which consumed huge amounts of wood annually.

In the baths, slaves also served as masseurs, rubbing patrons with olive oil before they exercised or after they had visited the caldarium, then scraping oil and dirt off with a curved piece of metal called a strigil. This passed for ablutions in an age without soap. An afternoon at the baths usually ended with a foray into the *frigidarium,* where a pool of cool water offered a refreshing finale. The sequence, wrote the physician Galen, was intended "to warm the substances of the entire body, to loosen them up, to even out their differences, and to relax the skin and clean out whatever has accumulated under it."

At the Stabian Baths, it was also possible to swim in the *palaestra,* or exercise yard. Serious athletes, however, may have gone instead to Pompeii's largest exercise ground, the Great Palaestra, a three-acre sports facility hard by the Amphitheater at the city's east-

Eerily intact almost 2,000 years after its last use, this hot steam room served men in Pompeii's Forum Baths, one of three such large establishments in the city. Patrons normally brought their own bathing tools, seen inset opposite. The set includes a small metal pot for oil that was rubbed on the body, scrapers called strigils to remove dirt and sweat, and a shallow pan used for interim splashes of cool water. The floor was so hot in the caldarium, *or hot room, which was located next to the boiler room, that bathers had to protect their feet with special clogs.*

ern end. Its open court, punctuated by a large pool, was surrounded by columns and planted with venerable sycamores. Here could be found on any given day weightlifters, broad jumpers, discus hurlers, bowlers, runners, javelin throwers, swimmers, and boxers—a motley crowd of fitness buffs no doubt making a considerable ruckus, as is evidenced by the Roman writer Seneca's grousing about the noisiness of the exercise yard in the nearby town of Baiae. Teachers sometimes convened classes under the porticoes of the Great Palaestra, and food vendors catered to calorie-starved athletes.

Parts of the Great Palaestra were destroyed by American warplanes during World War II. The Germans had established command posts and fortifications near Pompeii—important targets for the Allies pushing north to Rome. Amedeo Maiuri, director of excavations at the time, sent urgent messages to U.S. commanders pleading with them not to bomb near the site, but in September of 1943 planes appeared overhead. Accompanied by an assistant, Antonio Jorio, the director pedaled toward Pompeii in a mad bid to salvage what he could, but before reaching the city he was blown off his bicycle by the concussion of an exploding bomb. Maiuri suffered only an injured leg and went on to investigate Pompeii until he retired in 1961 at the age of 75. Jorio disappeared in the bombing.

Just east of the Great Palaestra, sport of a very different kind was staged at the Amphitheater, a large elliptical structure tucked up against the city wall. This was a place of institutionalized violence—not unknown to spill over into the stands. In AD 59, reported the historian Tacitus, "there was a serious riot between the people of Pompeii and Nuceria, a nearby town. It all started with a small incident at a gladiatorial show. Insults were hurled, then stones, and finally swords were drawn. The locals from Pompeii came out of it best—a number of Nucerians were taken off wounded or dead." In a mood to clamp down on hooliganism, the Roman Senate voted to close the Pompeian Amphitheater for 10 years, a serious blow to the sports-crazed populace.

In the early days of the empire, noted the Roman writer Vitruvius, gladiatorial meets were held in forums. Those in Pompeii must have gained renown throughout the area, since the amphitheater erected to replace the forum as a venue was given a seating capacity of 20,000—Pompeii's estimated population. An inscription

A stylized wall painting shows men fighting during the notorious riot at the Pompeii Amphitheater in AD 59 as well as many details of the 460-foot-long Amphitheater itself, including the masonry arches that supported the outer walls, the staircases leading to the upper rows of seats, and the velarium, *or awning, that could be stretched over the crowd as protection against the sun.*

preserves the names of the officials responsible for building the stadium: the duumvirs Valgus and Porcius. This and details of the stonework helped August Mau date the structure to roughly 80 BC. Though relatively unsophisticated compared with later structures, the Amphitheater is the oldest surviving example of its type. The construction technique allowed for tiers of raised seats: High arches bolstered the outer walls, and exterior staircases added further structural support. On hot days, awnings were strung to keep the audience shaded, an amenity that warranted advertising. Read one inscription touting an upcoming event: "The gladiatorial troop hired by Aulus Suettius Certus will fight in Pompeii on May 31. There will also be a wild animal hunt. The awnings will be used." Officials received front-row seats, around the walled arena, while the middle seats went to those willing and able to pay for a ticket. Admission to the crowded upper tiers was free.

A meet began with a procession of gladiators, each specializing in a particular mode of battle. The bareheaded *retarius* carried a fisherman's trident, a dagger, and a net. The helmeted *thrax* bore a short sword or curved dagger and a round shield. The *equites* fought on horseback, the *andabatae* blindfolded. At Pompeii, crude graffiti, paintings, and bas-reliefs on tombs exhibit fighters in such outfits, and a few remains of costumes were dug up in the gladiatorial barracks near the old Triangular Forum.

After the opening procession, mock fights between combatants wielding wooden swords whetted the audience's appetite. The real contests followed, with pairs of gladiators facing off while music played and crowds roared. The gladiators might also be pitted against wild boar, bulls, or bears. Battles between lions, panthers, and other animals were also popular; the hapless creatures were goaded into ripping each other to shreds.

Although a fight between gladiators was technically to the death, valiant losers might be pardoned. Contrary to the Hollywood interpretation, thumbs-down actually meant that the victor should drop his weapon and let the loser go; thumbs-up meant drive the deathblow home. Slain combatants were dragged off by a hook through a portal called the Gate of Death, while the winners were crowned with bright ribbons and handed a purse. Fighters that were especially successful, wearing an aura of ferocity and courage that spoke powerfully to the Roman heart, became celebrities. One tavern near the Amphitheater prominently displayed a statuette of a smiling gladiator with his shield and sword, and merchants around town sold oil lamps embellished with the portraits of famous fighters. If a gladiator survived three years in the ring, he was released and granted a kind of immortality in public memory, as was Severus, winner of 56 bouts, and Auctus, of 50.

While prowess in combat generated some of the excitement of these spectacles, the spilling of blood was their essence. The practice of gladiatorial combat was ancient—probably once a funeral ritual of the Etruscans, who had dominated central Italy before the Romans. The Etruscans believed that an offering of fresh blood supplied the deceased with energy for the afterlife. The Romans did it for their own pleasure; death fascinated and thrilled them. Gladiatorial battle was for them a kind of performance art.

Romans nonetheless honored their dead with much ceremony, cremating them and ensconcing them in splendid graves. The Pompeians sited their tombs along the busy roads leading into the city, as though to mingle the departed with the living. The expressive nature that produced urban inscriptions and graffiti in such abundance showed itself in these roadside cemeteries. Tombs bore homilies, bas-reliefs of hunting scenes, lengthy statements describing the departed's station in life, and in at least one case a message that seemed to be addressed to wayfarers passing by: "This monument was made for Marcus Caecilius. Stranger, I am pleased that you stop at my resting place. Good luck and good health to you; may you sleep without a care."

For Pompeians, veneration of the dead entailed less sorrow than celebration of life's riches. So, on that fateful day in AD 79, at least a few among the city's population would have had plans for outings at the town cemeteries, where they would have lighted lamps in memory of departed loved ones, adorned graves with floral swags, and feasted together in full view of unquiet Vesuvius.

A GOD AT EVERY TURN

In 1978, at an ancient cemetery just outside Pompeii, excavators discovered the ash-shrouded form of a young girl who, fleeing Vesuvius' violence, had sought refuge among the tombs. Asphyxiated by the sulfurous gases, she died clutching a small sacred statue she had grabbed as she ran from home. The terrible anonymity of her untimely death fades somewhat in the light of this final gesture: She had turned to her gods in the desperation of her fear. Perhaps, with her last breaths, she had uttered a prayer to the family deity she held, promising offerings of garlands and sweet spices for her salvation; or, noting the unnatural dark of the sky and the hallowed grove in which she found herself, she may have invoked Diana, Roman goddess of the moon and guardian of the fields (above).

Whatever her parting devotions, the urgency of her faith calls out with arresting immediacy. So it is throughout the tragic preserve of Pompeii: The vigor and variety of the city's religious life endures, timelessly replayed in its temples and sacred byways. Near a fountain on the Via dell'Abbondanza stands an altar dedicated to the city's protectors, still bearing the charred remains of a sacrifice interrupted by Vesuvius' blast. In the richly appointed sanctuary of the Egyptian goddess Isis, the final devotion of the priests is recorded in their agonized death forms, scrambling to save the temple's precious objects.

By a quirk of fate, the eruption caught Pompeii at a time of great spiritual change. As a gateway south and east to Greece and Egypt and the Eurasian landmass beyond, the city was heir to a panoply of faiths. A host of foreign gods had begun to usurp the positions of the venerable Olympian deities and the imperial Roman pantheon. Christians were likely to have been here as well, although the evidence of their presence is sketchy. Their belief in a better world to come—which they shared with a few other so-called mystery cults—no doubt offered them some comfort even as the ashes fell.

HOMAGE TO THE IMPERIAL GREATS

Ever since they were granted Roman citizenship early in the first century BC, Pompeians made a practice of thronging to the northern end of the Forum every January 1 to celebrate the Roman New Year. Adorned with garlands and bearing laurel branches, they gathered near the Temple of Jupiter, a magnificent structure perched on a foundation 10 feet high *(background)*, to watch the sacrifice of a bull to Jupiter Optimus Maximus, god of gods and patron deity of Rome. To the proconsul's prayers for the safety of the state, the pious no doubt added their own silent petitions. Their godly duties to Rome fulfilled, the worshipers then reveled in games, feasting, and drinking.

Like all good Romans, Pompeians regularly paid homage to the official gods of state, especially Jupiter and the divinities associated with the spirits of the emperors, living and dead. But their fealty to these holy ones seems to have been perfunctory at best. When the earthquake of AD 62 devastated the Temple of Jupiter, the Pompeians did little to restore it. Instead, they cobbled together a makeshift temple from the humble sanctuary of Jupiter Meilichius, patron deity of Pompeian farmers.

Perhaps better loved was the state goddess Fortuna Augusta, divine guardian of the deceased emperor Augustus. As the goddess of abundance, Fortuna was associated with the poor; her priests were culled from the lowest classes, providing one of Pompeii's few avenues of social promotion. Her tiny but exquisite shrine, situated just a few yards north of the Forum, was veneered in marble. Though badly damaged in the earthquake, it was faithfully reconstructed, suggesting that the worship of Fortuna was more than just obligatory.

Neither love of ceremony nor social conscience motivated the Pompeians' piety toward the newest of their state gods—the reigning emperor, Vespasian. In a pragmatic bid to win his favor and his assistance after the earthquake, the citizens erected a temple in his honor. But the cynical Vespasian, immune to flattery, did nothing to help the ravaged city. Years later, he mocked the practice of emperor worship as he lay dying, saying, "Alas, I think I am becoming a god."

In existence less than 17 years when it was buried in the eruption, this altar stood before the steps of the Temple of Vespasian. Its bas-reliefs may depict the sacrificial rites performed in the consecration of the shrine itself.

This bronze statuette of Fortuna (near right)—originally known as Divine Providence but associated latterly with the emperor Augustus—graced a special niche. The six-foot terra-cotta Jupiter was moved from the badly damaged Temple of Jupiter after the AD 62 earthquake.

73

POMPEII'S SPECIAL PROTECTORS

From their vantage atop the bluff overlooking Pompeii's Marina Gate, the masons trimming stone for the new Temple of Venus must have had a harrowing view of Vesuvius disgorging its hideous column of debris. Whether they watched for a while in hopeless terror or were among the first to run for safety, no one will ever know. Only the blocks they left behind remain to testify to their interrupted labor.

When the eruption struck, the temple's foundation had barely been laid. On its north side, excavators found several uncut stones, only waiting, it seemed, for the workmen's return. A statuette of Venus retrieved from the grounds—probably carried as a votive offering to a temporary chapel established there—helped identify the place as sacred to the goddess.

Had the builders finished the shrine, it would have been the third Temple of Venus erected in the century and a half since the victorious Sulla, Pompeii's Roman conqueror, first pledged the city to her. The Pompeians themselves tore down the first structure, a clumsy edifice of volcanic rock, and replaced it with one of marble. When the earthquake destroyed this, the people determined to raise an even more glorious temple to their protectress—who, as the goddess of love and nature, commanded the heart of this pastoral, sensual town. Her image was everywhere throughout Pompeii: on tavern signs, in shops, in villas, in gardens, and in gladiators' chambers.

By tradition, Venus shared her guardianship with Apollo, lord of all civilization, and Hercules, the city's mythical founder. Also toppled in the earthquake, the Temple of Apollo *(background)* was one of the few shrines to be fully restored; in keeping with the flamboyant tastes of the time, its damaged columns were stuccoed over in red, blue, and yellow, and were topped with ornate Corinthian-like capitals. Few traces remain of what is believed to have been a temple dedicated to Hercules. But numerous statues and paintings of the ancient hero in gardens and alcoves attest to the townspeople's enduring affection for him.

A marble Venus (near left), *her breasts covered by a painted golden bra, removes a sandal while balancing on the head of the fertility god, Priapus. Apollo the Archer* (far left) *draws back his now-missing bow. The statue once stood before the god's temple* (background illustration); *a replica occupies the spot today.*

Hercules clutches a club—his weapon of choice—in this three-foot bronze statue, which once adorned a large peristyle garden in a villa on the southwestern side of Pompeii. Because he traveled widely in the course of performing his famous 10 labors, Hercules was thought to offer protection on long journeys, and so was venerated by merchants and traders. The oldest of Pompeii's special guardians, he was worshiped in many household shrines.

ANGER OF THE LITTLE GODS

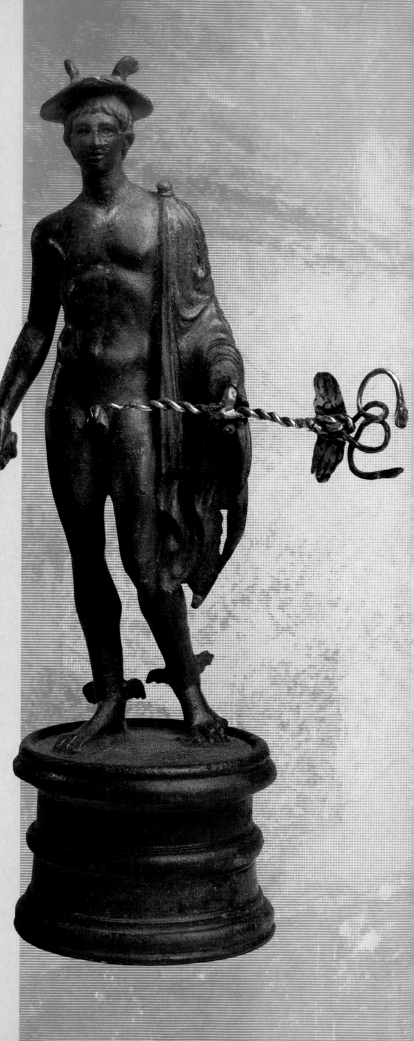

Toward the end of the evening meal, in grand and humble dwellings alike, pious citizens propitiated the spirits of hearth and home with the same ritual: The father would rise from the table and, draping his toga over his head, approach the family shrine with a small tray of offerings—perhaps a scattering of grain, a bit of salt, a wine-soaked crust, a crumble of cinnamon. These he would place on the altar and, with palms upturned, utter a prayer for the family's well-being. The others would then pour libations and drink in homage to the "little gods."

This done, all could rest well. Like Romans everywhere, Pompeians regarded these domestic deities—called Lares and Penates—with utmost seriousness. Along with the *genius,* or advising spirit, of the house, these exacting gods demanded ritual devotion in exchange for guardianship of the family and its possessions. Their shrines, known as *lararia,* took many forms: a simple wall niche, a painting representing the deities, or a miniature templelike wall mount with statuary. In some homes, such as the House of Menander *(background),* images of ancestors shared the altar with the figurines of the Lares and Penates; in others, family relics and personal mementos—clippings from a first beard, say—were kept there.

Failure to properly celebrate the household gods could have dire consequences. In fact, Pompeians feared it was the widespread neglect of such religious duties that had precipitated the great earthquake. Perhaps in conciliation, the penitent inhabitants erected the Temple of the Lares on the Forum soon after that catastrophe.

But the most telling evidence of devotion lies elsewhere. As the terrified Pompeians fled their homes during Vesuvius' eruption, at least a few remembered to take their protectors with them: Archaeologists have found nine of the little statues lying in the streets.

Often, the figure of a traditional Roman god stood on a household altar alongside those of the familial deities. Mercury (right), the fleet-footed god of commerce, was an appropriate choice to watch over the homes of wealthy merchants.

In this shrine from the House of the Vettii (left), the home's guardian spirit is flanked by two dancing Lares. The serpent symbolizes earth deities and the procreative powers of the master of the house.

Balancing on the balls of his feet, a Lar—measuring only 11 inches tall—pours a sacrificial libation from a drinking horn onto a dish. The Lares had always been known as general protectors of home and family; their kindred Penates had originally been guardians of the storeroom.

A FAITH STEEPED IN MYSTERY

A short walk from the Forum, where the regular Pompeian streets gave way to narrow, curving alleyways, stood the Temple of Isis. Normally, the worshipers of the Egyptian goddess celebrated their exotic rites hidden behind the temple's high walls *(background)*. But every March, when winter's storms ceased to roil the sea, Isis' secretive devotees spilled out of their enclave and headed toward it in a grand spectacle known as the Procession of the Boat. Leading the pomp were white-robed priests carrying an ancient bark over their heads. The believers, costumed in fantastic Egyptian dress, thronged behind. Once at the water's edge, the priests launched their holy vessel, symbol of the craft that, according to Egyptian myth, ferries the sun on its nightly underworld voyage to the dawn—and rebirth.

Beginning in the late second century BC, sailors, slaves, and merchants from the known corners of the world had introduced such myth-based cults, or mystery religions, to Pompeii. Isis claimed the largest following. The Procession of the Boat was only part of a sacrament based on the resurrection parable of Isis, goddess of heaven, and her mate, Osiris, god of the sun. According to the myth, after Osiris was dismembered by the god of darkness, Isis searched for his remains, which were then reassembled and resurrected. Worshipers reenacted the event through elaborate rituals, striving to capture such immortality for themselves.

Priests led two services daily: one at sunrise, to glorify the risen Osiris, and another at two o'clock in the afternoon, to sanctify the water of life *(painting, opposite, above)*. Although much about the liturgy of Isis must be guessed at, the last moments of temple life are known in tragic detail. When Vesuvius blew, the priests abandoned their meal of eggs and fish, still on the stove, and bolted from the sanctuary, grabbing ceremonial treasures as they ran: a silver urn, a statue of Isis, ritual vessels. The men were found on the temple grounds, some crushed under columns and others asphyxiated, their precious objects clasped in their hands.

A sacred ibis (near right) *once hallowed a wall in the Temple of Isis. Destroyed by the earthquake but immediately rebuilt, the temple comprised a central shrine surrounded by an initiation hall, lodgings for priests, and a chancel containing sanctified Nile water.*

When shaken, an Egyptian-style sistrum (right) *emits a rattling sound that, along with the ringing of cymbals* (above), *formed the ritual music of Isis worship.*

The blessing of holy water from the Nile, performed daily at the temple, is depicted in this Pompeian wall painting. Flanked by acolytes and sphinxes, a priest at the top of the steps offers for adoration a vial of the sacred liquid—Isian symbol of fecundity and rebirth. Followers stationed along the steps join in worship as a second priest fans a sacrificial fire at an altar before which ibises wander. To the lower right, a pipe player accompanies sistrum-wielding priests in the assembly.

Recovered from the colonnade of the Temple of Isis, this marble figure is the only image of the goddess to survive the volcano intact. Fashioned in the Archaic Greek style, the statue held a sistrum, now missing, in its right hand. Dangling from the left hand is an ankh, the Egyptian symbol of life.

ECSTASIES OF WINE AND LOVE

When Allied bombs fell near Pompeii in 1943, some of the city's most prized buildings were damaged. But by a lucky stroke, the explosions also unearthed the ruins of the Temple of Bacchus, lost sanctum of the only mystery cult to rival that of Isis. Devotees of the god of wine celebrated an ecstatic sensuality that at times shocked even the most tolerant of Romans.

The structure of the temple reveals something of the practices of these cultists. Beside the altar archaeologists uncovered two vast stone *triclinia,* or reclining couches. After a long period of fasting, worshipers gathered here for a banquet. As acolytes in goatskins poured wine for the supine celebrants, a priest—naked except for a crown of grapes—performed a sacrifice. Drinking and feasting followed, interspersed with ritualized dance that, as the heady effects of the sacramental wine took hold, grew increasingly frenzied. The revelers eventually achieved an exalted state in which they believed themselves released from mortality.

By participating in such Bacchanalia *(background),* the cultists were pursuing communion with the mysteries of fertility, reproduction, and seasonal death and rebirth. In southern Italy, where Bacchus was associated with the native deity Liber, liberator of inhibitions, such celebrations may have been orgiastic. Thought to promote lawlessness, Bacchic worship was banned by the Roman Senate in 186 BC, but evidently with little effect on the Pompeian cult, which flourished up to the time of the eruption. The popularity of this faith is most apparent from the number of its symbols—ivy leaves, maenads, satyrs—found represented in Pompeian gardens. Some archaeologists even suggest that in Pompeii, where the line between the secular and the sacred was thin, every garden was a temple to Bacchus.

Looking rapturous even in decay, this mask of a maenad—a female devotee of Bacchus—once adorned the end of a ceremonial chest or coffer from Pompeii. The cult was particularly popular with women, who were said to freely abandon themselves to the drunken, sensual worship.

Two Bacchic revelers—a satyr (near left) with a staff and goatskin, and a maenad waving a torch and drum—lose themselves in an ecstatic ritual dance around a shrine.

As depicted in this Pompeian statuette (right), a tipsy, bloated Bacchus carelessly spills out the contents of his drinking amphora. A more imperial portrayal (below) shows the god, clad in a gown of purple grapes, guarding the vineyards of Vesuvius. Part of a lararium painting, the image was probably intended to protect the wealth of the owner, who may have made his fortune in wine.

A PANOPLY OF IMPORTED GODS

In 1938, while excavating the House of the Four Styles, off the Via dell'Abbondanza, the archaeologist Amedeo Maiuri made a startling find: An ivory statuette of Lakshmi, Hindu goddess of fertility, beauty, and wealth *(near right, below)*. That the voluptuous carving had made its way from India to Italy presented Maiuri with a quandary. Had some gadding Pompeian adopted the eastern Venus during his travels, or was the lovely Lakshmi the devotional object of a resident Hindu engaged, say, in Pompeii's textile trade?

Either possibility was conceivable. Increasingly, Pompeians themselves were turning to foreign beliefs. And under Rome's tolerant yoke, the city's population of tradesmen and immigrant slaves practiced their native religions with impunity. Exotic and darkly seductive, these imported faiths included the fertility cult of the Near Eastern mother goddess Cybele—which required novice priests to castrate themselves—and the harsh sect of the Iranian sun god Mithras.

Among the most popular of these strange religions was that of the Near Eastern deity Sabazius. In 1954, excavators discovered a colonnaded garden containing a humble masonry altar beside which stood two terra-cotta vessels, and storerooms housing talismanic sculpted hands and numerous bronze lamps. From the symbols on the hands and vases *(background)*, investigators ascertained that the garden was a shrine to Sabazius.

Scholars have reconstructed the rites probably enacted there by studying the writings of Clement of Alexandria, a Sabazian devotee from the second century AD who later became a Christian. In a typical ceremony, fennel-crowned worshipers danced as a naked priest struck them with a serpent. Then, in an action symbolizing death, he washed them with mud and bran, and guided them in the chanting of verses empowered to bring about a spiritual union with Sabazius. The ritual took place at night, under the flickering light of bronze lanterns.

Found in Pompeii, this ivory figure of the Hindu fertility goddess Lakshmi testifies to the diversity of faiths practiced in the city. An important commercial trading center, Pompeii was regularly exposed to exotic influences.

A bronze image of the Near Eastern fertility god Sabazius (right) represents him wearing a hat wreathed with grapes—possibly suggesting a connection with the god of wine, Bacchus.

In the palm of the bronze hand at right sits the god Sabazius, surrounded by a variety of mysterious symbols. This and the terra-cotta urn in the background illustration—used for drawing lots for initiations or for holding sacrificial offerings—came from a dwelling now known as the House of the Magic Rites.

THE POMPEIANS AT HOME

Disturbed by the excavators' spades and picks, a colony of small lizards scuttled across the ruins, some quickly disappearing into crevices and others settling again to bask in the Mediterranean sun. But a reptile of another sort remained behind, its scales glinting and its scarlet eyes ablaze with the first light that had touched it in nearly 1,800 years. The serpent, a coiled creature of gold and rubies, had been wrought by a long-vanished jeweler to adorn a lady's upper arm. Its owner must have treasured it, for she died attempting to carry it to safety when Vesuvius erupted and blew her world apart.

Her name was Cassia; the inscribed golden ring still clinging to one skeletal finger announced this to the men who found her, in the atrium of her ruined home. A few prized possessions—other ornaments, a family seal—lay nearby. She was a woman of wealth and importance, the member of a prominent family, dwelling in a mansion that was already centuries old when time stopped in Pompeii.

The unearthing of Cassia and her neighbors—and much of what they owned—revealed in rich detail the private life of the city. Within the rubble of their homes lay evidence of the personal tastes, daily routines, and domestic intimacies of its citizens. The archaeologist Matteo Della Corte, a leading figure in the excavations throughout the first half of the 20th century, was particularly noted

Gazing across 19 centuries of time, the Pompeian lawyer Terentius Neo and his wife seem to reflect on life in this fresco that once greeted guests entering their house. He rests his chin upon a scroll; she displays wax tablets and a stylus.

for combining scholarship and inspired guesswork to build up dossiers on individual Pompeians. Through such clues as graffiti on walls, notices of elections, labels on wine jars, inscriptions on tombs and statues, and the seals and jewelry found near the dead, he was able to make connections between people and the places where they lived.

The implications were not always clear. Names found in one context would turn up unexpectedly in another; illegible letters, local slang, and the ambiguities of first-century Latin raised as many questions as they answered. A lady called Primigenia, for instance, appeared to be the object of attentions from all directions: "Here's to Primigenia—most sweet, most lovable! Hail!" "With what joy of the eyes have we admired Primigenia!" Because the name was relatively common—it means "firstborn"—these and several other tributes could have referred to different women, but the similarity of the comments was certainly intriguing.

In 1932, Della Corte found a Primigenia mentioned in a scrawled line at the entrance to an aristocratic mansion known as the House of Menander, which was owned by relatives of Poppaea, wife of the emperor Nero. Some of the wording was obscure, but the import of the message seemed to be that anyone looking for a Novellia Primigenia could find her where she lived, in the nearby town of Nuceria. Twenty-three years later, Della Corte found another inscription that dispelled his early suspicions about Primigenia's character. In a cemetery near the Nucerian Gate, he deciphered a little verse dedicated to her. Again, the words allowed of more than one translation, but they apparently represented the lament of a lovelorn admirer for an unreachable lady. The writer wished that he might become "the gem set in your finger ring so that when you use it to seal a letter, I may bestow kisses on your lips." One could conclude that only a great beauty of unimpeachable reputation would prove so inaccessible.

Whatever the truth about Primigenia, there could be little doubt about the moral and social standing of the lady Cassia. Her remains were discovered by scholars from the German Archaeological Institute, who began excavating the house in October of 1830, in the presence of August von Goethe, son of the famous poet. To honor their guest and his father, the Germans named the site the House of Goethe; it was later renamed (incorrectly) the House of the

In the process of being excavated and restored, a house in Pompeii is seen with its peristyle and adjacent frescoed rooms lit up by the photographer. The ghostly shape of the original formal garden remains in the soil of the court, covered by a grid that enables archaeologists to record spots where objects or plant remains were found, as marked by the labels.

Faun, after a statue of a dancing human figure with pointed ears, later identified as a satyr, found in the atrium.

One of Pompeii's most imposing residences, the House of the Faun—which encompasses 3,600 square yards of living space—covers the entire extent of a long and narrow city block. Starting at the main entrance on the short southern side—where a mosaic set into the pavement spells out a Latin "welcome" in small pieces of red, white, green, and yellow marble—the German archaeologists slowly worked their way inward. Two years later they finally reached the rear of the property, but parts of the house stayed buried for almost seven decades more. In 1900, excavators found the remains of four people and two cows huddled together in a stall, just one or two rooms from where Cassia herself had fallen.

Over the years, the house yielded up its treasures. Cassia and her kin took obvious pride in the antiquity and elegance of their dwelling, which at one time had belonged to the venerable Satrii family, whose origins predated the Roman domination of Pompeii. (Cassia's people were probably not members of the Satrii clan: Evidence suggests that Sulla's nephew had taken over the property around 80 BC, doubtless breaking a longstanding chain of inheritance.) The house had been constructed early in the second century BC, and although some internal alterations and improvements were made, each generation had carefully preserved the architectural and decorative intentions of the original builders. Other wealthy householders might choose to follow restless fashion, but the owners of the House of the Faun apparently saw themselves as custodians of a historic monument. Even when the earthquake of AD 62 destroyed much of the town and triggered a spate of rebuilding along more modern lines, the Faun's occupants resisted change. They might repair a roof or restore a fading mural, but they stayed loyal to the past—and to the aesthetics of the architect who had executed his commission to such good effect.

No other house in the city displayed so perfect an example of the influence of the Hellenistic Greeks, who had put their cultural stamp on the area when Rome itself was still a backwater. The layout was logical and uncluttered, the rooms generous in their proportions, the perspectives pleasing to the eye.

In its internal arrangements, the House of the Faun followed a pattern that would suit Pompeians to the end. They built their homes according to an inward-looking plan that allowed them to take advantage of the kindly climate, at the same time guarding their privacy and maximizing security. In most houses, the door from the street opened into a narrow vestibule that led to a rectilinear arrangement of wings, open courts, porticoes, small chambers, and corridors. Some sections of the building might incorporate a second story, while other parts stood open to the sky. At the entrance to a typical house lay the atrium, a partially roofed court with a pool to catch rainwater, surrounded by an assortment of smaller rooms. (The main atrium of the House of the Faun extends more than 50 feet.) Beyond the atrium, if space allowed, many owners added a peristyle—a colonnaded courtyard, built to a traditional Greek design. Here the Pompeians deviated from the Hellenistic practice: Instead of paving over the central ground, they made of it a garden, often with a fishpond or a fountain in the middle. The wealthiest householders might not stop at a single atrium or peristyle, extending their residences with two or more.

A helmetless Alexander the Great (above), *in a clash of spear, sword, and hoof, spurs his mighty Bucephalus against Darius, turbaned king of the Persians, who turns in his chariot to face his nemesis from Macedonia. The mosaic masterpiece, composed of 1.5 million tiny stones, covered a floor of Pompeii's House of the Faun. The damage on the left probably dates to the earthquake of AD 62.*

    In decorating the walls of their house, the Satrii family had adhered to a conservative approach that the archaeologist August Mau, in his analysis of the city's artistic trends, labeled the First Style. The effect was austere but handsome. Stucco walls were divided into raised panels and painted; the subtle coloring and trompe l'oeil rendering of pattern, enhanced by the play of light from doorways and openings in ceilings, created an illusion of marble. Other elements of adornment, some perhaps added by later generations, showed greater flair. No other mansion boasted a more splendid collection of figurative mosaics: a set of theatrical masks symbolizing Tragedy in a lush botanical background; varied scenes of animals, from cats and

doves to sea creatures; a pointed-ear satyr and a maenad—a female devotee of the wine god Bacchus—locked in lustful embrace.

But no single artistic rendering in all of Pompeii was to make so profound an impression as the floor mosaic shown here, discovered early in the second year of the House of the Faun's excavation. On October 24, 1831, diggers reached the *exedra*—a large room open on one side and set between the house's two peristyles—where they uncovered a battle scene, meticulous in detail and dramatic in its impact, composed entirely of tiny, cut colored stones called tesserae. It was a work whose power leaped across the ages; other mosaics on a similar theme had survived from the classical period, but none could match this new find in its energy and skill of execution.

Initially, the picture defied identification and was understood only as a conflict between two unknown kings—one probably a so-called barbarian and one Greek. The first leaned over the side of his chariot and the second was on horseback, armies clashing around them. But the image was no simplistic glorification of military mayhem. It was charged with the emotions of the protagonists, facing their own deaths and struggling to save their comrades in arms.

Within a few months of the mosaic's unearthing, a trio of Italian scholars provided a more precise interpretation. The image showed a crucial battle in the conflict that had decided the fortunes of a large part of the ancient world: the war between the Persians, led by Darius, and the forces of Alexander the Great, seen here mounted upon his legendary stallion, Bucephalus. Goethe, learning of this conclusion and studying drawings of the mosaic that had been sent to him by a friend, agreed with the Italian analysis. "There may

A TROVE OF SILVER
IN A COUNTRY VILLA

"Enjoy life while you have it, for tomorrow is uncertain," reads the inscription on a silver cup *(right)* found in a Pompeian country villa. Circling the vessel, animated skeletons appear in scenes that illustrate the prophetic advice. The cup, one of a pair, was part of a 109-piece silver collection discovered during the 1895 excavation of the Villa Pisanella in the country region called Boscoreale, about two miles from Pompeii. Consisting of a full table setting as well as a few display pieces, the silver had been hidden in a vat in the villa's wine-press room. Lying next to the vat was the skeleton of a woman who perhaps had concealed the treasure, hoping to reclaim it later.

In Pompeii, as in Rome, silver was the metal of choice for luxurious tableware. Influenced by pieces plundered during military campaigns in the east and by wealthy citizens who paid high prices for such objects, Roman silversmiths set up shop to supply the demand. They created elaborately sculpted cups, bowls, pitchers, vases, ladles, plates, and porringers as well as toiletry items such as hand mirrors. Increasingly, those who could afford such luxury bought pieces and passed them down as heirlooms; one dish in the Pisanella collection was already about 300 years old when it was in use. Eventually, high output from the silversmiths meant that even ordinary households might own

Dark humor surrounds this cup on which skeletons, each inscribed with the name of a famous philosopher, act out scenes from life. Above left, a skeleton labeled Epicure greedily grabs a cake.

one or two pieces, but a collection the size of the hoard found at the Boscoreale villa could have belonged to only the very rich. Soon after the discovery of the villa's silver, Count Edmond de Rothschild purchased the set for an amount equivalent to about $1.5 million today. Two years later he donated the entire collection, including the pieces shown here, to the Louvre.

This wine pitcher probably graced the villa's table at special dinners. Among the figures decorating it are a cupid and a winged Victory sacrificing a deer.

Fruit-bearing olive branches, a popular motif in Roman art, embrace a dual-handled cup. The sumptuous detailing and molding show uncommon sophistication of technique.

Used solely for display, a silver-and-gold bowl highlights a figure (above and right) symbolizing Rome's African province. She wears a headdress of an elephant's trunk, tusks, and ears. A cornucopia indicates the area's abundance.

An elegant hand mirror (below) is one of the few silver toiletry items in the collection. On the back are Leda and the swan, well-known figures from Greek mythology.

well be no question," he wrote in March 1832, "that the mosaic depicts Alexander as conqueror and Darius among his troops, overcome and himself constrained to flee." "It is the most royal picture in the world," declared the German scholar Ludwig Curtius.

Despite its artistic treasures, the House of the Faun was no museum, but the residence of a wealthy family who enjoyed its comforts. Space in Pompeian homes was always at a premium, yet here there was room enough for the domestic services—latrine, workshops, gardeners' sheds, and storage chambers—to be relegated to a separate corridor, or ranged along the rear of the complex. Among its other amenities, the Faun contained the earliest private bathing rooms to be found in Pompeii—equipped with an under-floor heating system—and a particularly spacious kitchen, high-ceilinged and well endowed with windows, for the release of smoke and cooking odors.

In this typically small Pompeian kitchen, charcoal fires were built atop the masonry hearth, the focal point of meal preparation. Bronze pots with curving bottoms could be nestled down in the coals for the greatest heat absorption. A window over the hearth allowed smoke to escape; some kitchens also had an opening in the roof.

On days when Cassia's family chose to give a dinner party, these quarters hummed with activity. A large brigade of household slaves—the family would have owned dozens—stood ready to cook the feast, prepare the public rooms, and generally make life pleasant for hosts and guests alike. Among the leisured upper classes of Pompeii, such entertainments were an important obligation. Dinner parties began at three or four in the afternoon, after the guests had made their ritual visits to the baths, and could last far into the evening. Sociable Pompeians often occupied a quarter of their waking hours in convivial dining, punctuated by a little gambling, a board game, or a performance by slave dancers and musicians hired for the night. In some circles, literary discussions were common.

The House of the Faun possessed four dining rooms, used according to the time of year, the weather, and the number of guests. On a hot summer's day, diners might enjoy the airy chamber that opened on one

side to the peristyle. In cool weather, the meal might be served in a more sheltered dining room, well lighted by large windows and floored with a mosaic on a suitably seasonal theme: the spirit of Autumn, personified as a cherub with a crown of vines, astride a lion and quaffing deeply from a golden bowl.

At dinners and banquets, men and women reclined side by side on broad, sloping couches arranged in a U-shape around a low, central table; they might also take their food from trays set on small, round, three-legged tables. Etiquette was scrupulously observed, although the dignified master of the House of the Faun—no records indicate whether this was Cassia's father or her husband—would never have resorted to the ploy of one of his contemporaries, perhaps a man less secure in his social standing, who inscribed a code of conduct on his dining room walls. "Do not be coarse in your conversations," enjoined this host, whose residence accordingly earned the name House of the Moralist. "Do not cast lustful glances, or make eyes at another man's wife." "Restrain yourself from getting angry or using offensive language. If you cannot, go back to your own house."

The guestlist for gatherings at Cassia's home doubtless reflected a broad social mix. Like other leading citizens of the day, the host would happily mingle friends of his own rank with merchants and tradesmen, former slaves he had liberated and helped set up in business, the ambitious sons of these freedmen, and other so-called clients—citizens of modest circumstances who regarded their host as a patron and benefactor. However heterogeneous the company, on formal occasions a strict limit was most likely imposed: The Romans deemed nine diners to be an ideal number, allowing three people to each couch. Even so, the dining room could easily get crowded, what with the comings and goings of servants and the presence of additional slaves brought along by many visitors to attend to their personal needs.

If the appearance of his house is anything to go by, the master of the House of the Faun was a man of refined sensibilities and something of a traditionalist. He followed convention, serving his guests a meal that

A Pompeian cook used utensils like those shown below to feed a household: a flat bronze bowl, a red-clay bowl with cover, an iron grate resting on an iron tripod used to grill meat or fish, long-necked clay jars for spices, herbs, or oil, and a bronze baking pan for small cakes.

was elegant rather than excessive. Everything was designed for easy consumption with spoon or fingers. There was no need for such exertions as cutting up meat: Slaves performed this task behind the scenes. After its journey from the kitchen, the food would be less than piping hot, but portable braziers stood ready in the dining room for reheating, or to prepare the final flourish in front of the guests.

Often the first course consisted of an assortment of small savory items, bearing more than a passing resemblance to the modern Italian antipasto, and traditionally including eggs and olives. If Cassia and her kin were admirers of Apicius, a Roman gastronome of their century whose collected recipes have survived into modern times, they might ask the cook to prepare one of his specialties as a main course: perhaps a fresh ham seasoned with a mixture of dried figs, honey, and bay leaves pressed into slits in the meat, then baked in a pastry crust. Beef was eaten far more rarely than pork or lamb; goose and game birds were popular. With the Bay of Naples on their doorstep, Pompeians also had a variety of fish to choose from, and served the local catch in a multitude of pungent sauces.

Roman palates appreciated strong flavors—hearty additions of pepper, aromatic spices such as cumin, and the more assertive herbs such as lovage, bay, and thyme. Many dishes mingled sweet and sour; a typical sauce for poultry or game birds required pepper, toasted cumin, damson plums, honey, vinegar, and myrtle wine. And few entrees tasted right without a liberal helping of *garum* or *liquamen*—intense, salty preparations based on a fermented amalgam of small fish such as anchovies and sprats, together with the entrails of mackerel and other larger species. Garum was a relatively thick, strong sauce; liquamen a lighter, strained version. Dessert, which in contemporary Latin parlance was called the second table, always included fruit and might run to a sweet cheesecake garnished with poppyseeds, or a cooked mixture of beaten eggs and olive oil, served with cracked pepper and honey on top. This delicacy—*ova mellita,* or honeyed eggs—has survived, in name only, as the omelet.

Only after the meal would guests settle down to serious drinking. The company might adjourn to another dining room, illuminated by several oil lamps made of bronze or clay, where slaves offered fresh supplies of wine. No one's cup remained empty for long. In a large storage room next to the kitchen in the House of the Faun was an ample stock of amphorae filled with what were presumably the owner's favorite wines, perhaps including an excellent

Preferring their wine diluted, Pompeians kept water handy in warming vessels as they dined. This bronze samovar-like urn, of superb workmanship, was of versatile design: It could be hung by the chains attached to the three female heads or stood on its three lion paws. An internal device allowed heating with coals. Carbon in the vessel suggests it was in use at the moment Vesuvius erupted.

Dolphins plunge in obeisance to bearded Triton and serve as lid handles for this ornate bronze food warmer. Double doors resembling those of a temple give access to the firebox. In winter, food warmers also helped remove the chill from drafty Pompeiun dining rooms. Side handles in the shape of hands allowed this one to be moved about easily.

local vintage called Vesuvinum. Few people drank wine undiluted. In chilly weather, they warmed it with a ladleful of boiling water; in summer, they liked it cooled and thinned with pure spring water.

More pretentious families than Cassia's might choose to regale their guests with a far more ostentatious spread, featuring costly delicacies from the farthest corners of the known world and ornate, labor-intensive set pieces composed of foods pretending to be whatever they were not. The Latin satirist Petronius, describing a dinner given by the fictional glutton Trimalchio in a seaside town not unlike Pompeii, notes such treats as wild boar with a flock of live thrushes in its belly; a hare transformed into the mythical winged horse Pegasus; pork cunningly fashioned to resemble a fattened goose garnished with fish and birds. In this portrait of Trimalchio and his friends, Petronius would have stretched the truth just enough to raise a smile from discerning Pompeian readers; they knew the sort of people he was talking about.

Pompeii had its share of the newly rich. Unlike families such as the Satrii, whose wealth was based on the ownership of land over many generations, these new men had made their money in trade and now sought to find a foothold among the local elite. One prominent member of this affluent class had probably, in his own small way, contributed to the success of dinner parties at the House of the Faun. His name was Aulus Umbricius Scaurus, and he was Pompeii's leading manufacturer of and dealer in fermented fish sauces. Many of the details of his private life and of his profession have been reconstructed from a variety of sources by the American classics scholar Robert Curtis, who has worked on the subject since the 1970s.

Perhaps because of its proximity to good fishing grounds, Pompeii was one of the empire's major sources of garum and liquamen. Pliny the Elder included it in a list of cities famous for their fish sauce. As one of the most important staples of the Roman kitchen, garum was big business. Usually bottled in small terra-cotta vessels, it could be found throughout the empire and was even carried by the legions on their campaigns. The painted labels affixed to these containers—which might identify, in addition to the contents, the manufacturer, the shipper, and the ultimate recipient of the goods—often bore the names of Umbricius Scaurus and his kin. Jars with the Scaurus label have turned up in various shops and households in Pompeii, in nearby Herculaneum, and as far afield as Fos-sur-Mer in southern France.

To satisfy the sophisticated tastes of his customers, Scaurus not only manufactured several different types of fish sauce at home but also imported foreign varieties for local sale. Labels on some vessels attest that they were delivered to Scaurus from a producer in Spain. As well as possessing his own shop, Scaurus had an interest, probably a controlling one, in at least half a dozen outlets elsewhere in the city. Jar labels found in Pompeii and its environs indicate that these premises were run by other members of the Scaurus clan. A sister or a wife, and at least two freed slaves who had adopted the family name, are listed on various consignments.

For his own children, Scaurus dreamed of higher things. He must have used his wealth to sponsor his son's career in politics, for the young man—who bore the same name as his parent—was elected to the office of duumvir, a post that he could never have achieved without financial backing. Scaurus Junior did not survive to enjoy this success for long: The family tomb, outside the city's Herculaneum Gate, displays an inscription put up his memory. Although his political tenure was short-lived, the younger Scaurus seems to have been held in high esteem by his fellow citizens. His father made special mention on the plaque that the city council had donated 2,000 sesterces toward his funeral costs and had voted to erect in his honor an equestrian statue—now vanished—in the Forum.

However great his wealth, and whatever social heights he attained, Scaurus Senior took pride in the way he made his money. His house, in the old quarter of Pompeii near the Marina Gate, was a handsome edifice of split-level design, with three atria, a fishpond in the peristyle, and a private bath on the lower floor. Parts of the building may have been 200 years old at the time of the eruption, but he, or his predecessors, modernized the house to suit the fashions of the day. Scaurus' tastes leaned toward the ostentatious. A conspicuous feature of the renovations was a personalized mosaic floor in the atrium adjoining the new main entrance: a decorative composition of black and white tesserae, most notable for four highly realistic representations of fish-sauce jars. Each container was reproduced in meticulous detail, down to its distinct hand-lettered label noting such things as contents, source, and its superior quality. All but one of the labels bore the name of Aulus Umbricius Scaurus himself.

The position of these mosaic vessels was carefully calculated to attract the eye. Scaurus clearly intended his guests to notice them, to walk around and scrutinize each label in turn and make the appro-

EATING AND DRINKING IN A CITY OF PLENTY

Pompeians liked good food, and thanks to the fresh ingredients of field, stream, and sea, and the exotic produce of other Mediterranean regions, they ate well. The day began with bread and honey with wine to dip the crusts in, supplemented perhaps by olives and dates. Lunch tended to be light, made up of eggs, bread, and cheese. Dinner was another matter. Eaten in mid- or late afternoon depending upon the season, it varied according to resources and the occasion. Although the poor had to content themselves pretty much with porridges of wheat, split peas, or broad beans, the rich could indulge a taste for spicy, lavish fare, especially if company had been invited to dinner.

Following custom, each guest arrived carrying a toothpick and a napkin to use during the meal, at the end of which the soiled linen might be given to the slave attendants as a tip. Since there were no forks—which meant that food had to be eaten with the fingers—a napkin was an absolute necessity.

A dinner of three courses could go on for hours. The first course, the *gustus,* might be shellfish and salad. It was followed by the meat course. A banquet could call for several kinds of fowl, ranging from dove, partridge, and pheasant to peacock, ostrich, and flamingo (absent a flamingo, says one recipe, a parrot will do). Fish might also figure on the menu, and there were close to 100 kinds for cooks to

choose from. After the meat course came fruit; then the heavy drinking began, with the finest wines bearing the vintner's name and the consulate under which the grapes were pressed (one favorite had aged 100 years).

Cooks drew upon a full gamut of recipes, some of them recorded by Apicius, one of the world's first cookbook writers. They included such delicacies as stuffed dormouse, an arboreal rodent, and snails fattened on milk. Among the most famous of Apicius' recipes was one for flamingos' tongues and mullets' livers. Woe to the cook who botched so extravagant a dish: He could be brought before the master and beaten.

priate exclamations of surprise and delight. The display would hardly have appealed to patrician sensibilities. According to Robert Curtis, "Scaurus and Trimalchio no doubt would have gotten along well."

It was only in this symbolic and somewhat tasteless form that Scaurus brought his work home with him: His processing plants and warehouses were located elsewhere. He saw his opulent abode as a place to spend and display wealth rather than acquire it. However, other Pompeians—not just humble artisans, but people higher up the social scale than Scaurus—made no clear separation between workplace and home. Even some of those living at the House of the Faun may have engaged in a bit of retailing. Along the front of the property were four shops, two with internal doorways giving access to the house itself, which would not have been the case if these premises had merely been rented out to some unrelated tenant.

One of the city's leading bankers, Lucius Caecilius Jucundus, undoubtedly used his home as an office. In his handsome residence on the Via Stabiana, he stored the records of his complex financial transactions. Excavators clearing rubble in 1875 found a chest bound with bronze containing 154 wax tablets, miraculously preserved through the destruction wrought by Vesuvius. These tablets revealed the monetary secrets, loans, and repayments of many prominent citizens of Pompeii—including members of Scaurus' fish sauce business—and gave historians invaluable insights into Roman banking practices.

Jucundus was the son of a freedman who had laid the foundations of a successful family business. One or both saw fit to pass on the gift of liberty to one of their own slaves. To show his appreciation, the liberated servant commissioned a bronze portrait bust of his former master and presented duplicates to him for display in the atrium of his house. An inscription on the pedestal of the one surviving copy identifies the donor and dedicates the work to his benefactor: "Felix, freedman, to the Genius of our Lucius."

Whether the bust is of Jucundus or his father, the man himself springs to life, his personality intact. Roman sculptors were generally skilled in realistic depictions but would sometimes tend to idealize features. This particular member of the craft, however, rendered the shrewd businessman's visage with unsentimental honesty. He spared neither the low forehead nor the wrinkles, nor the large, protruding ears that must once have been the bane of the schoolboy's existence. But he also conveyed the intelligence and the shrewdness of the gaze. From the look of him, this was not a man easily outsmarted in financial dealings.

The luxurious house on the Via Stabiana offered proof enough of Jucundus' business acumen. However humble his family's origins, Jucundus had acquired along with his fortune a taste for the arts. He commissioned a number of fine wall paintings, including one showing the aftermath of the Trojan War, when King Priam retrieves the body of the slaughtered hero Hector. Vesuvius' eruption ravaged the work, but a fragment of the scene survives, showing the aged but still lovely Queen Hecuba looking down on her dead son from a window, grief writ plain upon her face.

For some Pompeians, their property itself provided a source of income. One entrepreneur who sought to make her living in this manner was a woman named Julia Felix, owner of the largest house excavated to date in Pompeii. Covering more than twice as much land as the House of the Faun, the building occupies an immense square block of the city just across the street from the Great Palaestra and the Amphitheater; its northern side faces onto the Via dell'Abbondanza. Despite its urban setting, scholars have described it as a villa, primarily because of its formidable size. Within its precincts, the sense of space must have indeed suggested that of a rural retreat. The property included elegant living quarters, a large garden complete with a fishpond and a handsome portico with slim rectangular marble pillars, an eating house, baths, shops, and a cluster of dwelling quarters for hire with separate entrances. On the day of the volcano, a large notice on an outside wall near one of the entrances advertised the facilities for rent: "In the landed property of Julia Felix, daughter of Spurius, may be rented a bath fit for Venus and suitable for respectable persons, shops, rooms on the floor above, and apartments, from the

A tripod table rests on an exquisite floor of marble with a border of animal figures. The table was found in a tablinum—*a kind of reception room between the atrium and the garden peristyle, or courtyard. An array of delicacies for guests was set out on tables like this.*

An oil lamp on a tall and slender standard gave dim and smoky illumination to Pompeian nights. This one has a single nozzle for a wick; other lamps, however, had up to 14 nozzles, increasing light but also adding to the smoke.

A bronze bench with well-wrought legs would have been more inviting with its customary cushions. It was known as a bisellium, or "seat of double width."

next ides of August until the same date recurs for the sixth time, that is for five consecutive years. When this quinquennium has elapsed, the lease may be renewed by simple agreement."

Had Vesuvius not intervened, Julia Felix would have been pleased to guide prospective tenants around the premises. But nearly 1,700 years would pass before anyone came looking. And those who did, in 1755, were a band of treasure hunters more interested in easily plundered valuables than in the design or decoration of the house. The party dug through the heaps of debris and carted off such prized objects as a set of fine wall paintings representing Apollo and the Muses, which later found a home in Paris, at the Louvre. In their frantic hunt for salable souvenirs, these first excavators ransacked the place and left it worse off than it had been before.

For nearly 200 years, the ruins again lay buried in rubble. The little that was known about them gave rise to ignorant rumors about the property's function. Unaware that many of the objects found there were fertility symbols and that other evidence appeared obscene only to their own prudish sensibilities, some early observers created a myth based on such items as the advertisement of a "bath worthy of Venus," an enormous carved stone phallus, and graffiti left by dozens of short-term visitors—including one named Phoebus, who gave his occupation as male prostitute.

In 1952, the Italian archaeologist Amedeo Maiuri—who had overseen the excavations during most of the middle years of the 20th century—undertook a second and far more meticulous investigation of the site. He treated both property and proprietor with considerably more respect than had been shown by his 18th-century predecessors. Although little was known of Julia Felix, other than the evidence of her exquisite taste as seen in her elegant house, she was undoubtedly a businesswoman, keen for profit. Some scholars assume that she must have been an heiress who had fallen on hard times and was forced to let the family mansion. Her father's name—

Spurius—suggested humbler origins, but this is by no means certain. Whether she had inherited the villa or bought it herself, she clearly saw it as a valuable investment.

To this day, scholars dispute the use of the property. Maiuri's research indicated that the "bath worthy of Venus" was not some watery playroom for devotees of the goddess of love, but a small public facility that Julia had constructed for sound commercial reasons. He believed that after the earthquake of AD 62 had put many of the city's larger baths out of action, Julia saw a gap in the market and filled it, providing all the standard features, from changing areas to cold-plunge and steam rooms.

Matteo Della Corte, in contrast to Maiuri, felt that the property was the headquarters of an organization known as the Young Men of Pompeii. They set up their own gymnasium on the premises, with all the usual exercise equipment. Lawrence Richardson, an American classicist at Duke University, put forth yet another interpretation in 1988, proposing that the house was originally built as a bath and eating club for businessmen. Either way, those who frequented the place felt free—in typical Pompeian fashion—to leave their autographs on any available blank surface. Pursuing his special interest in ancient graffiti, Della Corte investigated the names of these inscribers, cross-checked them against names found elsewhere, and managed to learn something of their social status. Some boldly identified themselves with their family names and professions, others hid behind nicknames.

Although there is no evidence that they were ever there at the same time, the inscribers apparently included young gentlemen and artisans, as well as other, humbler types. There was Campanus, a jeweler, and Aulus Vettius, possibly a scion of the rich merchant family that owned one of the town's grandest mansions; Priscus, who earned his living as an engraver, and Habitus, who was busy boring his friends with accounts of his success in some athletic games at Nuceria, held on April 21 in an unknown year.

Elsewhere in the villa, people did hire chambers for short stays. Couples left records of their visits: For example, Pithia Prima dallied here with someone who called himself Sparitundiolus, which Della Corte translated as "bursting fish."

Whatever the goings-on among her tenants, Julia had fitted out her property to a luxurious standard. Maiuri's excavations revealed that she had adorned the residence and garden with hand-

POMPEII'S GARDENS OF DELIGHT

Citizens of the Roman Empire treasured their public, private, and commercial gardens, considering them essential to the good life. Pompeians in particular—who according to the poet Florus inhabited "the fairest of all regions, not only in Italy but in the whole world"—spent every possible moment in the green retreats that lay at the heart of their homes.

The largest houses sometimes boasted several elaborate peristyle gardens—graceful colonnaded oases, open to the sky, where owners could relax to the sound of gurgling fountains and admire the marble and bronze statues set among the plants. Even tiny houses had their small plots.

In formal gardens, evergreens predominated, with only a few flowers providing spots of color. In less formal ones, fruit and nut trees spread shade. Vegetables and herbs flourished as well, blessed by a temperate climate that permitted at least three crops a year. On special occasions, lavish, elaborately wrought garlands of blossoms and fruit were suspended between the columns. This form of decoration was much imitated by wall painters in interior rooms *(above)*.

Of the gardens studied in Pompeii, one of the most thoroughly examined is an expansive plot measuring 115 by 123 feet at the southeast end of the city *(below)*. Called the Garden of Hercules, after a marble statue of the deity found there during the first excavations in 1953-54, it seemed unusually large for a modest house. Its function became clear when later digging—involving the application of several ingenious archaeological methods *(overleaf)*—revealed that the plants raised there for at least part of the year were the basis of a thriving industry.

In an aerial view of the Garden of Hercules, the house (lower right corner) *is dwarfed by the plot itself, dotted with cement casts made by archaeologists of cavities in the soil.*

AROMAS OF THE PAST

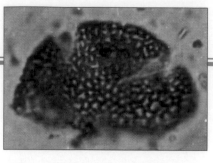

Deciphering clues gathered from the debris of Vesuvius, the world-renowned Pompeian expert Wilhelmina Jashemski spent more than 35 years reconstructing the histories of the city's gardens. Her research enabled her to describe in remarkable detail what the gardens produced, how they were tended, and even the varied purposes they served.

In solving the mystery of the Garden of Hercules, for example, much of her detective work focused on the study of soil contours and carbonized plant remains, and on making casts of hollows in the ground left by decayed roots and stakes *(below)*. The casts served almost as fingerprints, revealing that several large trees, including a cherry and an immense old olive, once thrived within Hercules' walls. The absence of tree or plant cavities in much of the rest of the garden

indicated that most of it had been planted in flowers or vegetables, whose decomposed roots would have been too small to leave spaces big enough for volcanic debris to fill. This conclusion was strengthened by the evidence of great numbers of cavities where stakes had supported sun covers to shade young plants.

Ancient pollen grains were found in samples of soil that Jashemski sent for testing to Professor G. W. Dimbleby at the Institute of Archaeology, University of London. Although experts had insisted that no pollen could have survived the heat from the volcanic fallout or the passing of the centuries, Dimbleby identified 21 different kinds of pollen grains. Weed pollen was almost entirely absent, one of several indications that the garden had been well tended.

Other signs of care included

Olive pollen, like this grain, from the Garden of Hercules helped confirm that the oil-bearing fruit had grown there.

an elaborate watering system with beds of varying heights to aid irrigation *(right)*. Indeed, the design of the beds, the generous size of the plot, and the results from her root and stake castings led Jashemski to believe that large quantities of flowers had been grown here, for purposes beyond personal enjoyment. Small glass vials recovered whole from the house and in fragments in the garden helped complete the picture. Jashemski deduced that Hercules' owners cultivated a host of blooms whose essences, when combined with oil from the olives and other essential ingredients, yielded perfumes and unguents that could be bottled and sold.

Found buried in volcanic debris, this hatchet, shown with a modern handle, may have been used to weed the wide flower beds of the garden (below).

Attempting to identify trees that once grew in the Garden of Hercules, Wilhelmina Jashemski and her assistants turned to the soil itself. First, the team extracted the volcanic debris that had filled up and preserved the cavities left by the decomposed roots (far left); next they inserted reinforcing wires; then they poured cement into the holes.

Days later, after the casts had had time to harden, the workers removed the surrounding soil, exposing, as in the photograph at near left, a faithful replica of an ancient root.

These perfume bottles, iridescent with age, helped Professor Jashemski conclude that the garden and adjacent building functioned as a perfumery. Excavation of the irrigation channels and the beds produced remains of glass vials and clay unguent containers. In the garden, a hoe blade, similar to ones still used in the area, turned up, and tucked away in a corner was a doghouse.

some marble and terra-cotta sculptures, including figures from ancient Greek philosophy, history, and myth.

Not all housing in Pompeii was built on so grand a scale as the villa of Julia Felix, nor so well stocked with art treasures as the House of the Faun. Most neighborhoods accommodated a social mix. Modest homes stood alongside noble residences, and many large mansions built for grandees of earlier ages who had since moved to country estates were subdivided into apartments for humbler families. This was especially the case after the earthquake caused a housing shortage within the town.

The multistory premises known as the House of Giuseppe II (in honor of Joseph II, emperor of Austria), for instance, had probably been the lavish base for a single wealthy family before the tremors of AD 62, but by the time of Vesuvius' onslaught it had been split up into several small dwellings and a shop. Any handsome plasterwork that had once adorned the atrium was stripped away, walls were torn out, columns removed, rooms subdivided, a cramped staircase inserted, old doors walled up, and a new one cut into the facade. The commodious bath—with niches, a fountain, and a circular window—where previous owners had once cosseted themselves in luxurious privacy was apparently turned into at least a semipublic facility. Another wing became a commercial bakery, with a workroom for mixing and kneading dough, and an oven far larger than any single family would require. Neighbors who had known the place in its days of glory might have shaken their heads at these symbols of its decline.

But the wealthy upper classes by no means enjoyed a monopoly on good taste. Even very modest houses were designed with an appreciation for architectural harmony. In one particular home a block east of the theaters, rooms were few in number but elegant in proportion; the entire building still exudes an atmosphere of intimacy and warmth. Its garden, overlooked by a two-story peristyle, must have been a peaceful haven, with a gracefully curved low wall enclosing the peristyle columns and forming a raised bed for plantings. Someone—perhaps the occupants themselves or a friend who had come to bask in their happiness—has written on the wall of the portico that "lovers, like bees, need a life of honey." As a result, the residence is known as the House of the Lovers. The city's gardens are full of similarly appreciative graffiti. Visitors knew they would please their hosts by leaving such tangible thank-you notes.

Pompeians loved their gardens and spent much of their time there, dining in summer on open-air couches under canopies or arbors, consulting the sundial, amusing their children with puppies and pet turtles, teaching caged blackbirds to sing. To honor their Lares and Penates—the ancient gods who protected hearth and home—they built shrines both within the house and in the garden, either simple niches or elaborate miniature temples, where burnt offerings were proffered at appropriate times.

Those modest citizens who had insufficient space for vine-clad pergolas, flowering bushes, paths lined with boxwood hedges, and splashing fountains would compensate as best they could. The priest Amandus cherished a huge tree that completely overshadowed his tiny courtyard; he must have taken pleasure in the song thrushes, warblers, turtledoves, robins, and swallows that would have visited its branches. His more privileged neighbors filled their spacious peristyles with trees bearing olives, walnuts, almonds, pears, apples, figs, and cherries. Some gardeners grew herbs and vegetables for the table. Other gardens were very formal, with low plantings of clipped box, rosemary, acanthus, ivy, and sometimes laurel or oleander.

The construction of the aqueduct by Augustus around the turn of the millennium had given the city increased quantities of fresh water. This allowed some owners to indulge in ornamental fishponds, fountains, and miniature streams. At the House of Octavius Quarto, for instance, a canal was built along a terrace and lined with small statues, including a miniature sphinx; the watercourse continued in the lower garden in playful imitation of the Nile. In other gardens, statues were turned into fountains, pouring jets of water into marble ba-

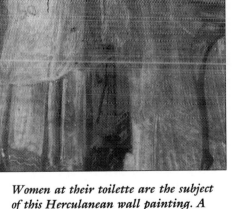

Women at their toilette are the subject of this Herculanean wall painting. A matron—who is depicted in the company of her daughters and a slave—wears a necklace similar to the gold, emerald, and mother-of-pearl choker seen here, a masterpiece of the jeweler's art.

sins; the palatial home of the Vettii brothers boasted 14 of these fountains in the peristyle, fed by an ingenious hydraulic system that still works today.

As part of her monumental visual survey of the ruins, the American archaeologist and ancient historian Wilhelmina Jashemski has spent more than 35 years in a detailed study of the city's gardens. Through a careful recovery of surviving pollen grains as well as carbonized seeds, fruits, vegetables, stems, and traces of root systems, she has enabled botanists to identify the plants that Pompeians grew for pleasure, for food, and—in some cases—for profit. Her methods for salvaging this material parallel those of the excavators who reconstructed the faces and figures of the eruption's human victims from the impressions left in the debris when their bodies decayed. The root systems of many dead plants, like human remains, also decomposed, leaving a clear impression of their shapes and structures in the form of cavities deep within the soil. Each garden site is first meticulously peeled down to its base level of AD 79, at which point these root systems become visible. The accumulated volcanic debris within the cavities is carefully extracted with special tools, the delicate networks reinforced with strong wire, and the spaces filled with cement to make a cast. After a few days, once the casts have hardened, the surrounding soil is removed, exposing a faithful reconstruction of the ancient root. With the information thus acquired, scholars have often been able to specify the precise plants grown and to re-create ancient gardens with examples of the flora that lived there before the eruption. Once again, roses bloom in the gardens of Pompeii.

What Jashemski could not glean from the analysis of roots and other physical remains she learned from the botanical imagery employed so lavishly in Pompeian art. Owners adorned their garden walls, as well as their inner rooms, with paintings. Jashemski examined small enclosed garden plots that were magically enlarged with painted gardens on one or more surrounding walls showing trees and statues too big for the actual garden. Two-dimensional peacocks strut and preen, and nymphs pour water into nonexistent basins. Painted orioles flutter above date palms, rosebuds, and the long, slender leaves of oleanders, all depicted with scrupulous accuracy.

Statuary was an essential element in a Pompeian garden, and owners often displayed painted sculptures, like those of the blond-haired boys with dolphins shown at upper left and at right. In the photo above, the peristyle garden of M. Lucretius is seen as it was found. Here, Silenus, a satyr, standing in his niche, pours water from a wineskin down the steps into a circular pool. Another satyr (foreground) inspects one of Pan's hoofs.

Even in their own time, these were transitory works of art. Every few years a Pompeian householder would pay to have scenes replaced because of fading that resulted from exposure to the weather. The layers of volcanic ash that buried the gardens protected those depictions they did not immediately destroy, but when excavation brought these works to light, little could be done to prevent them from deteriorating. In any case, they were frequently ignored in the hunt for more-obvious treasures.

In the course of her survey, Jashemski has often been able to record these doomed portrayals for posterity before they are lost forever, and to track down those described and noted in on-the-scene sketches, paintings, and photographs by previous generations of archaeologists. Yet such efforts have sometimes failed at the eleventh hour, as did her attempt to photograph a painting known from a drawing made by an earlier excavator—a charming scene of a fruit tree with four baby birds in a nest excitedly greeting their mother's arrival with food in her beak. "The previous year," Jashemski recalls, "we had worked our way through the overgrowth of saplings and branches that choked the garden and had peeled back enough of the vines to make sure that the painting was still there. When we returned the following year, we were told that the garden had been cleaned, and we hastened to photograph the painting. But when we reached the wall we found that this unique painting had been loosened by the winter rains and was a heap of plaster at the base of a bare wall."

Sheltered from the elements, decorations within houses stood a far greater chance of survival. Pompeians of all social classes covered their walls with painted images. Although rooms were typically very small—only 10 feet square for a *cubiculum,* or bedroom—murals helped relieve any sense of claustrophobia. Even relatively unassuming dwellings displayed their occupants' passion for the visual arts; few walls were left unadorned with vivid colors and painted borders framing some decorative image or dramatic scene. In those homes where slaves were fortunate enough to have their own bedrooms, the walls might be enlivened by patterns of stripes or simple sketches.

Then as now, styles changed and tastes differed. Members of the old patrician families, still living in their ancestral homes, saw no reason to meddle with the decorations that had pleased their fore-fathers. Others purposefully decorated in the early, traditional style. But there were others still with no attachment to bygone days—unsentimental modernists who thirsted for something fresh and different. The newly rich undoubtedly kept watch on the house next-door, to check up on any dramatic innovations and, where possible, outdo them. Besides these free spenders, however, there were many householders without the resources to follow fashion. In the years between the earthquake and the eruption, Pompeii seems to have slipped into a state of economic decline.

At the moment when the volcanic flood swept over them, the houses of Pompeii displayed a range of decorative approaches span-ning more than 200 years. Despite a succession of distinct trends, few elements were ever entirely abandoned. People mixed old-fashioned treatments with the latest look; motifs were borrowed, altered, dis-carded, and revived. The oldest mansions, which would have been regarded as period pieces by many of the last Pompeians, preserved the ancient practice of painting wall surfaces to imitate the textures of stone panels; even columns and cornices might be faked through artful renderings. Early in the first century BC, wall painters began to indulge wholeheartedly in illusionary techniques. They practiced tricks of perspective, leading the onlooker's eye into imaginary ex-tensions to the room, offering tantalizing glimpses of nonexistent courtyards and slivers of painted sky, or pretending that the wall had disappeared altogether to reveal a fictional outdoors. Some of their inspiration came from the painted back-cloths used in the local the-aters as well as those of Rome and nearby Neapolis—architectural frames for the fantasies played out by the actors.

Tiring of these visual sleights of hand, fashion-conscious Pompeians around the beginning of the first century AD took note of some of the new trends emerging from the court of their emperor at Rome: a more formal style, bold color schemes, the use of abstract geometrical and botanical patterns to contain small painted scenes. As the century drew on, the paintings grew more intricate and fan-tastical, possibly reflecting the changes in temperament among the imperial style setters at the capital. Throughout the empire, the cool

Artifice brings the outside world into Publius Fannius Synistor's bedroom in his villa in Boscoreale, outside Pompeii. A luxurious expression of the wealthy Pompeian's drive to impress his guests, these beautifully preserved frescoes—now installed in New York's Metropolitan Museum of Art—tease the viewer with details meant to re-create and expand reality. For all their grandiose pretension, the panels convey a sense of fun.

classicism of Augustus was gradually giving way to Nero's florid extravagances. Then, in the years just prior to the eruption, a few pacesetters introduced the radical new departure of covering their walls with mosaics or genuine marble claddings. Their motive was most likely aesthetic, but this may also have been a way to cover up the cracks in earthquake-damaged walls. Still, if Vesuvius had never dropped its curtain, the town's great store of painted treasures might have disappeared altogether, as the social climbers and the modernizers called the decorators in.

Spared from such a fate, the visual images that survive reveal the deepest sentiments of Pompeii's people. Those with cultivated tastes looked to the Hellenistic world as the fountainhead of all arts and learning. Educated Greek slaves tutored their children, and Greek physicians—either slaves or freedmen—attended them when they fell ill. Scenes from Greek mythology and history were favorite subjects for domestic art. The priest Amandus, for one, enhanced the dining room of his house with paintings of the hero Perseus rescuing the maiden Andromeda, Hercules in the Garden of the Hesperides, and Icarus falling from the sky. And all over the city there were scenes from the Trojan War since, in the wanderings of the exiled Trojans, the Roman people had found a myth for their own beginnings.

The artists who executed these works sometimes relied on their own creative vision. More often, they copied old Greek models or used pattern books, producing the equivalent of modern prints. At the lower end of the market, craftsmen worked fast and cheaply, delivering art to order for customers with less sophisticated tastes. One popular item in their repertoire was the undulating snake that guarded the shrine of the domestic gods. Many citizens liked to hold a mirror up to their world, decorating their homes with faithful representations of themselves, their children, animals, birds, and miscellaneous glimpses of ordinary life.

In their way, these details are the greatest of archaeological treasures, as crucial to an understanding of the past as any buried temple or emperor's tomb. Because life stopped here so suddenly, the prevailing atmosphere is one not of death but of suspended animation. Messages written on the walls of empty rooms seem to await an answer. In the House of the Vettii, on a column in the peristyle, a young man has scratched a greeting: "Actius wishes his dear mother Cossinia good health!" Perhaps, on that dreadful August day, she had read it and smiled before the ashes fell.

HOUSES RAISED FROM THE ASHES

How inviting is your house, O Albucius," inscribed a guest on the garden wall of one of Pompeii's fine homes. Similar words could easily have been written of any of the town's other gracious dwellings. Exhumed from layers of pumice and ash, some eerily intact, such houses suggest what domestic life was like for Pompeians of means.

Abutting one another in a city short on building space, the mansions nevertheless guaranteed the inhabitants privacy and peace. Tall, generally windowless walls kept out the noise of the street and deterred any burglars. Yet, thanks to openings of various sizes in the tiled roofs, even the smallest townhouses were rich in light, the essential element of an architecture that counterposed sun-drenched areas with pleasantly shaded rooms. The vista from the street entrance drew the eye through the bright, high-ceilinged atrium and the diffused light of the *tablinum,* or principal reception room, to the sunlit peristyle, a colonnaded garden; the

striking effect was often enhanced by colorful murals and intricate mosaics.

The rooms shown on the following pages have little furniture, for scarcely any survived the catastrophe. It was scanty in any event, including little more than wooden couches, cupboards, small tables, and screens. Shutters, doors, and draperies closed rooms against winter cold. Tallow candles or oil lamps lit up the night, and charcoal braziers of bronze, iron, or terra cotta supplied meager heat. But Pompeian houses were not designed for winter; they came to life in summer.

Even in ruins, the palatial House of the Faun *(above)*—named for the statue in its atrium pool—reveals the serenity and grandeur that made Pompeii's townhouses such sanctuaries from the hubbub of the city. Small wonder that in the searing tumult of the final day, many Pompeians took refuge in the cool recesses of their homes, whose thick walls had hitherto always buffered them from the outside world.

A SPACE TO AWE CLIENTS AND GUESTS

Sunlight and shade mingle in the lofty atrium of the villa of L. Albucius Celsus, scion of an old Pompeian family. The expanse of the chamber—the largest atrium in Pompeii—and the sedate fresco decoration accord with the room's function as a formal reception hall, intended to impress visitors with the owner's power and taste.

A short corridor at the far end connects the atrium to the street; doors at the sides lead to bedrooms. Terra-cotta spouts lining the ceiling opening channel rainwater from the inward-sloping roof gables into the shallow impluvium in the center of the floor. This pool once drained into a cistern beneath the mansion, providing a regular supply of fresh water for household use.

Some owners heightened the ceremonial air of the atrium by displaying busts of family members and death masks of ancestors in niches or along the walls. The patron's iron strongbox might also be placed in the atrium, often cemented into the floor, with offices for his business affairs close by.

A SETTING FOR THE MASTER

Seen from the atrium of the House of the Ancient Hunt, a now-nameless patrician's tablinum, decorated with murals, opens on his villa's small peristyle. Typically, such rooms were intended to enhance the prestige of the master, who would stand here each morning to receive favor-seeking clients crowded into the atrium.

In most houses the tablinum was the largest of the chambers around the atrium and provided the best overall view of the interior. Its name, derived from *tabula* (board), may refer to the room's early function as a summer dining space. The tablinum may once also have served as the master bedroom, screened from the atrium by curtains or a folding wood partition. As house styles changed and family life shifted to the more secluded rooms around the peristyle, the tablinum became a kind of formal living room, a place for receiving guests who were not admitted into the private quarters.

SPACES OF ELEGANT PRIVACY

Affluent Pompeians lavished decoration on even the smallest domestic spaces, like the cubiculum in the Villa of the Mysteries *(left)*, typical of windowless Pompeian bedrooms. Here, a mural with an architectural motif provides an illusion of space. The white section of the mosaic floor outlines the position of the bed, which in other cubicula might have stood in a small alcove or been built into a wall. Most cubicula contained no more furniture than a bed and a lamp; personal belongings were kept in other rooms.

A frieze of bathing women adorns the alcove of a bath *(above)* in the House of Menander. Unlike the public baths most Pompeians used, those in villas were usually large enough for only one person, like the *caldarium,* or hot bath, shown here, part of a three-room suite that included a cold bath and a *tepidarium,* a warm room used for massage and for oiling and scraping the body.

A TASTE FOR MOVABLE FEASTS

Wealthy Pompeians followed the Greek custom of eating from a central table while reclining on cushioned, sloped masonry couches known as *klinai*. These couches could accommodate three persons each, and thus made nine the ideal number for a dinner party.

Many houses had more than one *triclinium*, or dining room, allowing the owners to shelter from the weather—or take full advantage of it. The winter triclinium below shielded host and guests from the elements; shutters covered the windows on the coldest days. But in the house at right, meals could be taken outdoors in summer. Lying on couches not seen here, guests ate from a table with a fountain at its center and gazed upon the fountain shown, the sound of both adding gentle music to dining pleasure.

AN OUTDOOR ROOM INSIDE THE HOUSE

A sunlit garden complete with fishponds brings some of the beauty of the nearby Campanian countryside into the column-lined peristyle of one of the largest of Pompeii's dwellings, the House of Julia Felix. Although the owner rented out rooms along with her private bath after the earthquake of 62 AD, she maintained her spacious peristyle for personal use.

The colonnaded court of Pompeian mansions was a Hellenistic import (*peristyle* comes from the Greek *peri*, "around," and *stylos*, "column"), but the paved floors of the Greek original gave way on the Italian Peninsula to an earthen surface that was planted with greenery. For outdoor-loving Pompeians, such an open space surrounded by a shady colonnade functioned as a center of family activities of all kinds, from children's games to reading and spinning wool.

SEEING THROUGH THE WALLS

Many Pompeians went to great lengths to transform their gardens and peristyles into terrestrial paradises. Often, where space was at a premium, realistic murals depicting landscapes and wild animals opened vistas beyond the walls, as in this secluded retreat in the House of Ceius Secundus. To blur the line between the garden and the image of various predators and their fleeing prey, the bottom panel bears painted ivy and myrtle, with birds flitting about. And a painted fountain in the corner appears to empty into a real gutter at the foot of the wall.

Even less lavish homes than this one augmented their few trees and plants with paintings of larger gardens or of animal-filled landscapes reminiscent of the game parks of the emperors at their country estates. The grandest houses, particularly the villas in the nearby countryside, however, had less need of space-expanding illusion. There, perspective carried the eye down long panoramas punctuated by statues, pools, and fountains, and aviaries ensured that the air would be filled with birdsong.

THE MIRACLES AND MYSTERIES OF HERCULANEUM

His face intent and his body poised as if in flight, this bronze athlete found at Herculaneum conjures up the terror of all who tried to escape the doomed city.

Like his many predecessors, the Italian archaeologist Giuseppe Maggi, director of excavations at Herculaneum from 1971 to 1984, enjoyed nothing more than to be actively searching for new discoveries. But in May of 1980 he had a more pressing matter on his mind when he ordered a trench dug on the southeastern edge of the site. The operation, carried out not by trained archaeologists but by local workmen, was designed to protect the Suburban Baths, an impressive edifice that had been built directly above the city's waterfront, but which today stands 500 yards inland and 13 feet below sea level as a result of Vesuvius' activity. The trench was intended to draw off excess ground water that was threatening to inundate the structure. Aware that chance had played a large part in the unearthing of many of Herculaneum's treasures, Maggi urged the diggers to proceed with caution.

Within a few days, they had opened a channel about 3 feet wide and 20 feet deep in front of the baths. The work was continuing when, on May 21, Maggi heard one of the men exclaim, " 'O muorto!"—Neapolitan for "a dead man." There in the muck was a human skeleton—an unexpected and interesting find, but not especially dramatic. Soon thereafter, however, two more sets of bones were uncovered, and Maggi realized he had stumbled on something truly exciting.

In more than two centuries of excavations up to that date, only a dozen or so skeletons had been found at Herculaneum. The scarcity of human remains seemed conclusive evidence that nearly all of the town's inhabitants had managed to flee the destruction. But now a different picture emerged.

To the west of the baths, diggers eventually came upon a series of vaulted chambers built into the sea wall, where the town's fishermen had probably stored their boats and gear. As they slowly hacked through the hardened volcanic debris that had filled these storerooms, they encountered a pitiful sight: scores of skeletons sprawled in the final convulsions of a ghastly death. Forty had perished in one chamber, 26 in another, 12 in a third. Apparently heading for the beach and an escape by sea, they had taken quick shelter in the chambers, only to be asphyxiated as the first lethal wave of ash and gas swept down on the town; moments later, the thick tide of searing rubble had risen around them, interring them in a common grave. Altogether, more than 150 victims were recovered from this one location. Because of the obvious suddenness with which the end had come, Maggi found himself wondering whether indeed any of Herculaneum's inhabitants had survived the catastrophe.

Until this grim discovery, Pompeii had garnered the lion's share of world attention. After all, it was a much larger place, bustling with commerce, while Herculaneum seemed only a sleepy seaside town, its narrow streets unrutted by wheeled traffic, its walls bare of the graffiti with which the more strident Pompeians had publicized their businesses, aired their political preferences, and mocked one another. Although only a small fraction of Herculaneum has been excavated, this general picture matched a description by the Greek geographer Strabo, who several

Layered in time, an excavated portion of ancient Herculaneum's decumanus maximus—"main street"—reposes beneath the city that sprang up above it. Houses and shops flank the wide avenue—unrutted because it was open to pedestrian traffic

only—and at the far end, the entrance to the Basilica shows through an arch. Beyond, still locked in the hardened volcanic matrix that makes digging at Herculaneum so difficult, may be the as-yet-undiscovered Forum.

decades before the eruption had called Herculaneum "a place salubrious to live in." Perhaps it had served as a resort for rich Romans eager to escape the pressures and intrigues of the capital. Indeed, among the early finds were the ruins of mansions built above the beach, no doubt to take advantage of the fine views and sea breezes.

These houses and the artifacts they contained had piqued interest when Herculaneum was first chanced upon at the beginning of the 18th century. Confronted with the nearly impossible task of mining through more than 60 feet of volcanic rock, however, treasure hunters soon turned to Pompeii, where the pickings were easier. Archaeologists, too, gave precedence to the larger city, even though the digs at Herculaneum occasionally offered a more pristine glimpse of the ancient world. At Pompeii, many structures had collapsed and objects been damaged as hot pumice pelted the area and piled up over the course of a number of hours. Herculaneum had also suffered severe blows when the raging torrent of volcanic slag came rushing down from Vesuvius, toppling walls and knocking columns off their bases. But here and there the deluge had slowed as it made its way through the streets, so that it rose gently in places, leaving things almost precisely as they had been before. Many wooden objects and foodstuffs were carbonized by the searing temperatures, others only slightly charred, and where the temperatures were lowest, some items such as rope or leather survived almost entirely unharmed. As the volcanic matter solidified, it formed an airtight cocoon that effectively sealed all these materials against the ravages of time.

While the ruins of Pompeii were laid bare in grand style, efforts to exhume Herculaneum were hindered not only by formidable physical difficulties but also by opposition from the residents of Resina (later renamed Ercolano), the town that had grown up over the site. In 1980, with so little of the place explored and so many questions unanswered, it seemed that Herculaneum was destined to remain shrouded in oblivion.

But the unearthing of the skeletons lifted one corner of the shroud. For those experts who knew how to read the coded language of bones, here was a virtual chronicle of life in a provincial Roman town. Analysis of the skeletons not only shed light on the health, wealth, and social standing of the victims, but also provided fascinating biographical details *(pages 133-137)*. Herculaneum was at last

127

revealed in its ordinary human dimension. Even before these discoveries, the ruins themselves and the artifacts retrieved from them had offered tantalizing hints of the city's character. Its theater, for example, demonstrated the love of its inhabitants for the performing arts; the quality of its sculptured objects revealed the refined tastes of its citizens; the existence of a huge library of philosophical works at its most luxurious villa teased with the possibility of a notably literary atmosphere. These glimpses of lifestyles in Herculaneum, together with the finds of rogues and amateurs and scholars who have poked through the ruins over the years, have provided us with a detailed picture of the town and its inhabitants.

Herculaneum's cultural predilections were evident almost from the first moment of its rediscovery in 1709, at the bottom of a well shaft. Initially, it was apparent only that the well-diggers had stumbled upon some kind of magnificently bedecked public building from classical times; nearly 30 years later, the site was identified as the theater of Herculaneum. The marvels of the place were legion. Standing alone rather than built into a hillside, the semicircular complex had a seating capacity of about 2,500—half the size of the larger of Pompeii's two theaters but grand enough considering that the town's population has been estimated at only 5,000. It was lavish in its appointments and decorations, its proscenium faced with yellow, dark red, purple, and black marbles imported from far-flung corners of the empire, its tiered seats segregated for different grades of dignitaries, its topmost edge adorned with bronze statuary of emperors and city leaders. The structure and all the ornamentation had survived the eruption intact, except for a few statues that had been swept from their perches as the volcanic flow crested the rim of the semicircle and poured down over the seats and stage, eventually filling the entire bowl.

One of three fresco masterpieces uncovered inside the Basilica at Herculaneum, The Finding of Telephus *illustrates a naked Hercules recognizing his infant son. In classical mythology, the baby had been abandoned in the wilds of Arcadia (symbolized by the wreathed female figure in the mural) and suckled by a doe.*

At the entrance to the Basilica, realistic figures of the proconsul Marcus Nonius Balbus (top) and his son—shown here in closeup—honored the most prominent family in Herculaneum. The Basilica itself was one of many generous endowments made by them to the city.

The theater, however, did not survive its discoverers as successfully. The first of these, Prince d'Elboeuf of Austria, carted off almost everything that was portable and could be hauled up the well shaft. His successor, Cavaliere Rocco de Alcubierre, was even worse. Conducting the digging almost as if he were engaged in a military operation, he had the original shaft enlarged to facilitate removal of the theater's treasures. Using convict labor, he extended the excavations into the residential part of town in pursuit of more valued objects, demolishing houses along the way. At one location, bronze letters were torn from their mounting and tumbled into a basket without any thought to recording the inscription. After watching Alcubierre at work, the German art historian Johann Winckelmann angrily declared that the engineer "knows as much about archaeology as a shrimp about the moon."

But even Winckelmann—whose systematic study of artifacts would reveal so much about both Herculaneum and Pompeii—was not interested in preserving ordinary houses to learn more about the people who had lived in them. Like many of his scholarly contemporaries, he had been deluded by Greek sculptures he had seen into thinking that the classical world had been peopled by a race of near-perfect physical specimens—"men like gods." Confronted with a statue of Marcus Calatorius, a leading Herculanean whose likeness had been placed in the theater, Winckelmann was appalled. Could this figure, with its grim mouth, furrowed face, and wart under one eye, be what Romans really looked like? Winckelmann for the most part kept his eye trained on the more idealized forms that emerged.

Alcubierre continued to root for plunder—slowly, haphazardly, and destructively pushing his tunnels forward. By 1739 he had mined his way into two other public buildings, the Basilica and the Palaestra. Later researchers determined that when Vesuvius erupted, the Basilica was probably less than 20 years old, having been rebuilt after the earthquake of AD 62, which wreaked havoc on Herculaneum as it did on Pompeii. Alcubierre's excavations there were curtailed by protests from the residents of Resina, who feared that the tunnels would cave in and bring down their homes. But before the access passages were filled in, two French travelers were able to explore the building and reported that the interior formed a large rectangular hall with a central area set off by columns—a traditional Roman plan copied in early Christian churches, which consequently came to be known as basilicas. At each of the two short ends were apses, or curved recesses, bedecked with frescoes. One of the most splendid portrays a mythological scene from the life of Hercules, legendary founder of the town *(page 128)*. Another celebrates the triumph of Theseus over the Minotaur and was executed with such mastery that when Alcubierre first saw it, he exclaimed, "The artist surpasses Raphael." A third depicts the centaur Chiron tutoring a youthful Achilles, who for protection from his enemies had been dressed as a girl and raised in female company.

An inscription chiseled into a section of the architrave—a row of marble blocks above the columns—records that the Basilica was rebuilt with funds donated by the proconsul Marcus Nonius Balbus, governor of a Roman province and Herculaneum's foremost citizen and chief benefactor, who also financed postearthquake reconstruction of the town gates and walls. Statues of Balbus and inscriptions attesting to his largess and importance have been found at several sites throughout the city; at the Basilica, the entire Balbus clan was honored in marble.

Inside the building were statues of the women of the family— Balbus' wife, mother, and two daughters. The two girls are relatively plain-featured and unremarkable, their mother handsome but somewhat careworn. The grandmother's countenance is stern and unyielding, suggesting a rather forbidding temperament that, from appearances, she may have passed on to her son. Balbus himself and his son, Marcus Junior, are shown on horseback at the entrance to the Basilica. The sculptor rendered them in identical poses, but in his treatment of the faces he captured very different personalities. Tight-lipped and authoritative, the proconsul radiates not so much patrician pride as executive self-assurance—befitting a man whose family, so far as is known, had risen from obscure origins. By contrast, the son is slightly frowning, with the merest suggestion of a pout to his lower lip; he looks a touch unsure of himself.

Given the vividness of the depictions, some researchers have been tempted to further speculation. The Balbus household, perhaps under the grandmother's controlling influence, could very well have been a tense place, ruled with an iron hand and fraught with resentments. As supporting evidence, proponents of this view point to a motto inscribed on a wall of Herculaneum's most grandiose house, tentatively identified as the Balbus home. It reads, "Who does not know how to defend himself does not know how to survive."

After spending more than 10 years burrowing through the

The Shrine of the Augustales served as headquarters for an elite group who saw to the worship of deified Roman emperors. Here, behind a locked door, was found the skeleton of a man who had been left behind when Vesuvius erupted. He may have been a disgraced Roman politician, banished from his city and kept under arrest by the Augustales.

volcanic matrix that entombed Herculaneum, Cavaliere Alcubierre still had little knowledge of the town's extent and was becoming increasingly frustrated by the slow progress. In 1748 he transferred his attentions to the site that would soon be identified as Pompeii, but despite some early successes, he became disheartened there as well; a year later he resumed digging at Herculaneum. Fortunately for posterity, he was called to Naples on military business before his smash-and-grab campaign could inflict further damage. Although he remained in overall charge, day-to-day operations fell to a much more methodical and thoughtful investigator, Karl Weber, a Swiss engineer who had been employed by the Spaniards since 1735.

Shortly after Weber took over, well-diggers just west of Herculaneum unexpectedly came upon a perfect circular marble floor that was part of a garden belvedere—an observation post or place of contemplation not unlike a gazebo. This feature was common in suburban Roman villas, and Weber would soon have the privilege of investigating one of the most superb examples of these lavish country retreats ever found.

Villas were quite fashionable during the last century of the republic. Julius Caesar, for example, was in the habit of repairing to his estate near Baiae, a spa town with seaside amenities that, according to Strabo, catered to both the ailments of the sick and the pleasures of the sound. Cicero, who frequently expressed disdain for ostentation, nonetheless had three villas on the Bay of Naples, where his favorite relaxation—so he claimed—was to sit on the shore and count the waves as they came in. In the decades following the discovery near Herculaneum, a number of such dwellings were unearthed along the coast and in the countryside around Pompeii, but none would surpass this first one to be excavated.

For six years, Weber explored a labyrinthine complex of rooms and halls and courtyards, sometimes working on half a dozen tunnels simultaneously. Despite exhortations from Alcubierre to concentrate on the search for art objects, Weber took pains to make a detailed floor plan—dated 1754—of those portions of the villa he was able to reach. There was little doubt that he had found a residence worthy of some great noble: a colonnaded building with red-tiled roofs stretching more than 800 feet along the shoreline. Architectural details suggested that it had been built in the second or first century BC as a fairly modest atrium house and had subsequently been expanded, growing ever more grand. Toward the western end was a peristyle more than 300 feet long and 120 feet wide, with a pool down the center measuring 217 feet by 23 feet—as large as some of the imperial baths built later in Rome. According to Weber, this pool and other ponds, fountains, and baths on the property were fed by an ingenious underground hydraulic system, the exact details of which remain buried.

Besides providing a showplace, the large pond probably supplied fish for the table—unless, that is, its owner had succumbed to the Roman craze for raising ornamental fish. According to critics, this hobby had so besotted some nobles that they gave their finned pets names, adorned them with jewels, and wept when they died. Cicero deplored these *piscinarii*—"fishpond fanciers"—claiming that in their obsession they neglected affairs of state, worrying only when their bearded mullets refused to eat from their hands.

Foot by foot, Weber's team exposed the villa's secrets, hacking away in dank, slimy tunnels—a risky venture because of deadly subterranean gases that could be trapped within them. On August 4, 1755, in a Herculanean tunnel, a spark struck from rock by a pickax caused an explosion that terrified the workers. But the courage and persistence of those excavating at the villa were amply rewarded: By the time the site was abandoned, 90 statues in bronze and marble had been found, ranging from Greek philosophers and statesmen to gods, satyrs, and animals.

At one end of the main peristyle, flanked by a pair of spirited bronze deer, was a bronze figure of Silenus, leader of the satyrs,

SARA BISEL AND THE TALKING BONES

For years scholars had interpreted the rarity of skeletons at Herculaneum as evidence that most of its inhabitants had fled before the eruption. Then, in 1982, workmen digging a drainage ditch stumbled across dozens of skeletons on what had once been the town's beachfront. Fleeing toward the sea, perhaps with the idea of taking to boats to escape the avalanche of ashes, gases, and rock, panic-stricken Herculaneans had sought shelter inside stone boathouses lining the shore.

And there they were still, on the day the American archaeologist Sara Bisel first saw them. When Bisel was asked to go to Herculaneum in 1982 to analyze some of the bones, she hardly expected to give years to the work. Nor could anyone have guessed that dozens of skeletons would come to

light and that they would yield not only a wealth of information concerning the Romans' diet and health, but also personal details about the lives of individual Herculaneans. The opportunity to study such remains was unprecedented. As Bisel was to write: "Romans of ancient times cremated their dead. Ashes do not tell us very much."

During their long repose under more than 60 feet of volcanic material, some of them carbonized by the extreme heat, the bones had been well preserved by ground water that kept them from oxidizing. Once

exposed to temperature and humidity changes, however, they would deteriorate rapidly, and one of the world's most amazing archaeological treasures would be lost.

So Bisel had to work fast. Under her vigilant, hands-on direction, each bone was lifted from its resting place, cleaned with jets of water and a toothbrush, allowed to dry, then dipped in an acrylic solution to harden. Typically, Bisel took two days to assemble a smashed skull from a welter of bone fragments, gluing and wiring the disconnected pieces together.

Only then did she allow herself the luxury of intensive analysis of individual remains. For the next six years—10 months a year, six days a week—she toiled, bent over scores of skeletons that surrendered their long-locked tales of life and death.

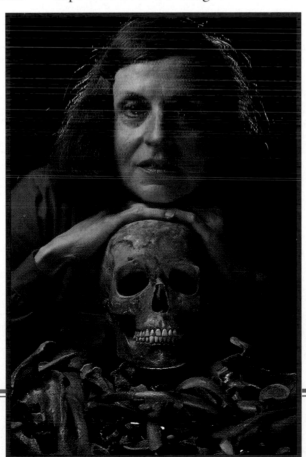

Sara Bisel, called the Bone Lady, rests her chin upon hands clasped over a 1,900-year-old skull, emphasizing her tender familiarity with the Herculaneans whose lives she wrested from anonymity.

RECONSTRUCTING LIVES FROM HEAPS OF PATHETIC REMAINS

"Bones are nice to feel," Sara Bisel once said. "They like to be fussed over, and they tell me their stories." By examining them, Bisel could determine a person's age and sex. Her measurements showed that the average Herculanean man stood 5 feet 7 inches tall, the woman 5 feet 1 inch. The flattening or thickening of some of their bones demonstrated the effects of nutrition, hard work, or exercise. One skeleton of a 16-year-old boy, with a well-developed chest, suggested a career as a fisherman, someone used to hauling on nets and oars. The youth's teeth were worn on the right side, probably as a result of his having held fishline in his mouth while repairing nets. By studying a female pelvis, Bisel could tell whether a woman had had children and how many she had had; each pregnancy left a tell-tale scarring of the bone.

Bisel even produced a health report on the citizenry. Their teeth, she wrote, were in better shape than those of contemporary Italians, thanks to a lack of sugar in their diet. Ridges on some teeth indicated childhood illnesses that had interrupted calcium absorption. Bisel's chemical analysis revealed that Herculaneans ate much seafood, as was indicated by a concentration of strontium in their bones. Some suffered from lead poisoning. Lead was used in cosmetics, pottery, and paints, but Bisel's guess was that these sufferers had developed their condition from drinking cheap wine—sweetened with syrup boiled in lead pots.

"She lay on her side, almost looking as if she had died in her sleep," wrote Sara Bisel of one skeleton. "As I brushed dirt from her left hand, something shiny caught my eye. It was a gold ring. When we uncovered the rest of the hand, we found a second ring. We ended up calling her the Ring Lady."

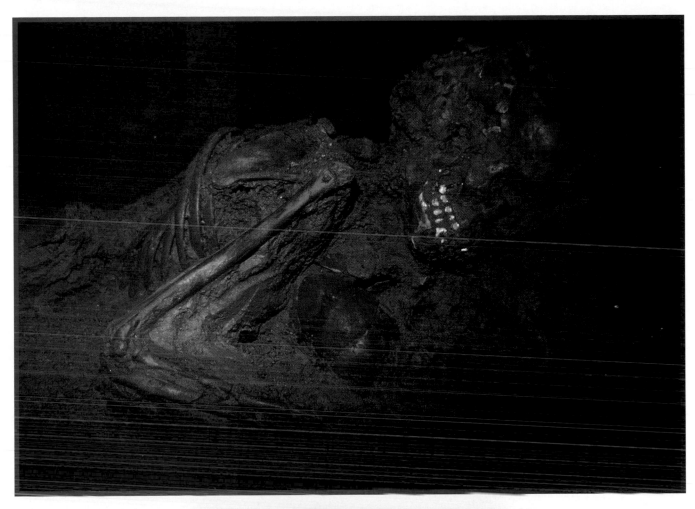

When the skeleton of a teenager was found curled protectively around the remains of a baby wearing a cupid pin and bells, some assumed it was a mother with her child. Bisel could tell from the girl's pelvis that she was too young to have given birth, and soon determined that the pair were a slave and her wealthy charge.

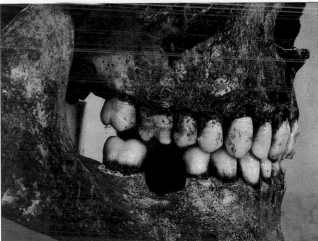

Ridges on the teeth of the slave girl told Bisel that she had eaten poorly or been very ill when a child. Her bones showed she had had to lift objects too heavy for her and had often run up and down stairs or hills. Two of her teeth had been pulled a couple of weeks before her death, leaving one of the gaps seen here.

THE SAGA OF A
ROMAN LEGIONNAIRE

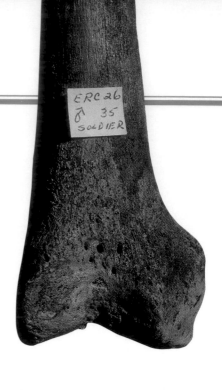

When the soldier fled to the shore, little could he have imagined that someday his bones would tell his tale. His skeleton was found facedown on the beach. His sword and scabbard lay beside him, and he had a set of carpentry tools on his back. About 37 years old, he had been muscular and well fed. Bisel had no doubt he had seen action. Six of his teeth had been knocked out, and he had been wounded in the left thigh, as an irregularity in the bone showed. He had probably served in the cavalry, for the bones near his knees had grown to accommodate the muscles needed to ride bareback. His forearms had been powerful, possibly developed from long sessions of practice with his

sword and shield and hours of hard manual labor. As all legionnaires were expected to have a trade in addition to soldiering, his tools—a hammer, an adz, two chisels, and a hook—were not surprising. He may have been in Herculaneum on leave, but, experienced trooper that he was, maintained enough self-possession during the eruption to collect his weapons and even a few coins, which were found beside him in a money belt.

A horseman to his very bones, the soldier had developed an enlarged area in the thighbone above his knee as a consequence of gripping his steed between his legs as he rode. The identifying label is Bisel's.

Among the gold coins found in the soldier's money belt was one (top left) struck with the head of Emperor Nero, who died 11 years before the eruption.

An archaeologist brushes the caked dirt of the ages from the soldier's skeleton. A sword, useless against the brute force of nature, lies beside the sprawling victim.

"When I examined the bone of his left thigh," reported Bisel, "I could see a lump where a wound had penetrated the bone and caused a blood clot that eventually had hardened." The lump is visible below Bisel's label.

Arms crooked, the soldier's skeleton lies on the gravel of the beach, his tool kit plainly visible on his back. Close by were found escape boats that the fleeing Herculaneans, overtaken by the volcanic cataclysm, had no time to launch. In all, Bisel studied more than 100 skeletons found in the area.

portrayed as a former athlete gone to seed, reclining drunkenly on a wineskin and snapping his fingers at convention. Not far off was the so-called Resting Hermes (the Greek version of the Roman god Mercury), whose lithe form has been reproduced in countless modern copies and is familiar the world over as the epitome of youthful health and beauty. At the opposite end of the pool was a life-size bronze of a sleeping faun, another masterpiece destined for universal fame. Near the center of the peristyle stood five female figures originally thought to be engaged in some sort of priestly dance, but who were subsequently identified as drawers of water. Nearby was a work that shocked its discoverers and was quickly locked away: a marble Pan engaged in sexual intercourse with a she-goat.

In sharp contrast to these displays of sensual beauty and gross indulgence, the long pool was bordered by marble statues and busts pairing Greek rulers with Greek men of intellect; the absence of comparable Roman examples suggests that the owner had little regard for philosophers or statesmen closer to home. Inside the house, more busts of Greek thinkers came to light: Demosthenes, the Athenian orator; Epicurus, who in the third century BC founded a philosophy that gained many adherents among Roman literati 200 years later; Hermarchus, student of and successor to Epicurus; and Zeno of Sidon, an Epicurean philosopher at Athens, who was one of Cicero's teachers.

From this illustrious gallery of Greek greats, it was clear that the villa had belonged to an intellectual. Proof came in 1752, when the excavators broke into a modest-sized room lined with shelves on which rested stacks of blackened cylindrical objects. The first guess was that these were rolled-up fishing nets or briquettes of coal. But when one of the rolls was accidentally dropped, fragments broke off, and the onlookers were astonished to see Greek writing in opaque black ink clearly legible against a slightly different background.

The material turned out to be charred scrolls of papyrus, and the room was a library—the first to be discovered from the classical

In 1754, Swiss engineer Karl Weber drew up this plan of the lavish Villa of the Papyri, sketching excavation tunnels carved through the 65-foot-deep volcanic matrix along with the layout, which includes an immense peristyle garden bisected by a fishpond. At far left is the small, round belvedere where workers digging a well first became aware of the villa's existence.

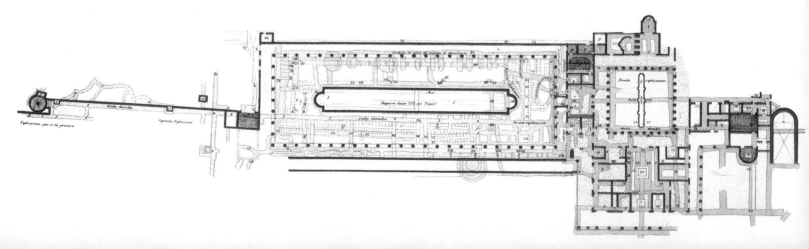

Complete with replicas of its majestic peristyle garden, fishpond, and statues, the J. Paul Getty Museum in Malibu, California, re-creates the Villa of the Papyri from 18th-century plans (below, left). The museum, which opened in 1974, houses Roman and Greek antiquities as well as works from the rest of Europe.

world. Perhaps, the scholars of the day wondered excitedly, these charcoal remains that crumbled at a touch were unknown works by the great Greek and Roman poets, dramatists, philosophers, and historians. With utmost care they were transported to the royal palace at Portici—just northwest of Herculaneum—where Camillo Paderni, director of the museum and artistic adviser to the Spanish king, Charles III, applied himself to the task of unrolling them. On November 18, 1752, he reported his results to the Royal Society of London, the world's foremost scientific institution. "Last month we found several very blackened paper volumes which, following the king's orders, I have tried to open without success. I am including a reproduction of a few words to give you an idea of how the ancients wrote." The outcome was a disaster, the loss irretrievable. Paderni had tried to slit open some of the scrolls lengthwise with a sharp knife, and although this method preserved the outside, the pressure of the blade crushed the brittle leaves within, destroying their contents forever.

More imaginative techniques were soon attempted, including treating the scrolls with vapors of mercury—a process that reduced them to a soggy pulp. In desperation, the Spanish court approached the Vatican, whose prefect recommended they enlist the services of Father Antonio Piaggio, a Latin scribe and superintendent of the Vatican Library's collection of paintings. Paderni—according to Winckelmann an "obstinate and ignorant man"—was furious at being replaced and jealously withheld the best of the scrolls, relinquishing only fragments. Nevertheless, there remained more than 1,800 scrolls in all to choose from.

Aware that direct manipulation would destroy the fragile documents, Piaggio constructed a special device consisting of a wooden frame strung with threads that would support the brittle papyrus sheets as they were unwound by means of a spindle turned by a screw. To prevent the scroll from curling back, the blank side was painted with a film of glue; for added strength, it was backed with goldbeater's skin—a tough, natural membrane—lined with silk. The work proceeded at an excruciatingly slow pace—at best, four or five hours to unroll just two or three inches. Despite Piaggio's efforts, some of the manuscripts were destroyed in the process. After four years, only three documents had been unwound.

The first proved to be a treatise on music by Philodemus, a first-century-BC Epicurean philosopher. Born near the Sea of Galilee, Philodemus had settled in Rome, where he became acquainted with such luminaries as Cicero, Virgil, and Horace. The discovery was a promising start, whetting scholars' appetites for the prospect of even greater literary treasures to come. But the other two scrolls were also works by Philodemus. In fact, the library was a collection of most of Philodemus' writings, along with a few other Epicurean works—including some by Epicurus himself—but none of the anticipated classical masterpieces. The disappointment was profound. "Do we not already possess many treatises on rhetoric," asked Winckelmann, "and is not Aristotle's Treatise on the Vices and Virtues worth more to us than all the rest put together?"

Over the centuries, *epicureanism* has come to mean unbridled self-indulgence, particularly in the pleasures of the table. As originally expounded, however, the philosophy was a good deal more austere. According to Epicurus, "It is not a succession of drinking feasts and of revelry, not sexual love, not the enjoyment of fish and other delicacies of a luxurious table that produces a pleasant life; it is sober reasoning."

Epicurus' rejection of voluptuous sensations was comprehensive. Love was dismissed as giving more pain than pleasure, and sex was frowned upon: "Sexual intercourse never did anyone any good," he gloomily warned his disciples, "and he will be lucky if it did not actually do harm." Marriage and politics alike were condemned as founts of strife. Believing that it was best to live in contemplative obscurity, classical Epicureans developed the metaphor of the gar-

Discovered in the Villa of the Papyri, a library filled with carbonized papyrus scrolls—among them, the six shown here (opposite, top)—tantalized scholars with the promise of works penned by the great ancients. All attempts to unroll the documents failed until an 18th-century priest, Antonio Piaggio, devised a machine (left) that accomplished the task, albeit at a very slow rate. Miraculously legible, the scrolls (right)—which are still being unwound, with the help of modern methods—appear mainly to be the work of Philodemus, an Epicurean philosopher, rather than classical masterpieces.

den, a spiritual refuge into which the wise man could retire, leaving the anxieties of the world behind.

By the first century BC, however, few Epicureans were practicing such an ascetic regimen, Philodemus himself among them. Besides his earnest philosophical tracts, he is credited with the authorship of lively, sometimes lecherous, epigrams and poems, including one to his mistress Philainion: "She is always ready for / Anything, and often lets / Me have it free. I'll put up / With such a Philainion, / O golden Cypris, until / A better one is invented."

To scholars such as Winckelmann, the collection of so many works by Philodemus suggested that the philosopher had owned the mansion, now known the world over as the Villa of the Papyri. But other researchers believed that the house was too palatial for a mere philosopher. They contended that it was more likely to have been the property of a wealthy patron.

One clue to ownership is contained in the writings of Cicero, who mentions an unnamed Epicurean philosopher as a great friend of Lucius Calpurnius Piso Caesonius—the wealthy father-in-law of Julius Caesar. According to Cicero, Piso was sadly lacking in the spirit of self-denial advocated by Epicurus. He lived for sensual pleasures, carousing with Greek boys and drinking from dusk to dawn. Cicero also accused Piso of having pillaged statues from Greece. Was this perhaps the source of some of the villa's artworks? Was the unnamed philosopher Philodemus himself?

Since Caesar's own country retreat was not far from Herculaneum, it is tempting to imagine him visiting his father-in-law at the Villa of the Papyri, the two of them strolling down the colonnaded pool, discussing the political situation and perhaps hearing Philodemus recite a poem in celebration of the meal that awaited them:

"Roses are already here, / Sosylos, and fresh peas, / And the first cut sprouts, and / The minnows that taste of / The surf, and salt soft cheese, / And the tender leaves of / Crinkly lettuce . . ."

Antonio Piaggio died in 1796, after almost 42 years of patient but essentially unsatisfying labor: The great lost works of antiquity were not among the scrolls he unfurled and deciphered. Despite the initial disappointment over their contents, however, the scrolls became collectors' items. In the 1820s, for example, the British envoy to Naples, Sir William A'Court, obtained 18 scrolls from King Ferdinand IV in exchange for the same number of kangaroos, a zoological oddity recently arrived from Australia. Some hoped, however, that the Villa of the Papyri contained a second library of Latin texts, since the Romans usually kept Greek and Latin collections separately. But in 1765 the residents of Resina once again forced Alcubierre to abandon excavations at Herculaneum. The shafts giving access to the villa were sealed, and all activity was transferred to Pompeii.

Although the glories of the actual villa were lost, they re-emerged in a new incarnation two centuries later and half a world away in Malibu, California. In a move that some critics considered pretentious and others inspired, the American oil billionaire J. Paul Getty chose the Villa of the Papyri as the model for a museum to house his collection of classical art. Using Weber's plan as a blueprint, American and Italian craftsmen replicated as much of the villa as was known, filling in the blanks with appropriate sections copied from other contemporary houses in Pompeii and Herculaneum. Every detail had to be authentic—from the marble, which Getty had imported from an ancient Roman stockpile quarried 1,800 years ago, to the herb garden, planted with 50 varieties cultivated by the ancients for their culinary, medicinal, religious, or decorative properties. Started in 1970, the

Excavated from a residence dubbed the House of the Stags, this marble statue—a transcendent example of Roman sculpture—is the first of two depicting a pack of hounds savaging a deer. In the second, the stag falls to its brutal attackers.

museum opened to the public in 1974, having cost Getty—who died without seeing it—$17 million.

Not long before Alcubierre's retreat, a Spanish architect named Francesco La Vega joined the endeavor and produced as complete a plan of Herculaneum as was possible from the available evidence. Later generations of archaeologists would put his map to good use, but for decades it remained little better than a curiosity, since the town lay essentially untouched. Eventually, after more than 60 years, work resumed in 1828. Partly because tunneling had proved so troublesome both physically and politically, those in charge decided to proceed by the open-trench system that was literally bringing Pompeii back into the light. Of necessity, this method limited available sites; only a few badly damaged houses were uncovered, and digging was halted once more after seven years. But the effort had its effects. Seeing at least portions of the ancient town out in the open, some people began to refer to its modern counterpart not as Resina, but as Ercolano—an Italian version of Herculaneum—as if they had finally made a connection with the past. The name was changed officially in the late 1970s.

Meanwhile, excavations at Herculaneum continued in fits and starts. In 1869, during the tenure of Giuseppe Fiorelli—one of the greatest archaeologists in Italy's history—the site was tackled seriously yet again. But technical difficulties and political turmoil closed things down only six years later. More than half a century would pass before the appointment of Amedeo Maiuri as superintendent of excavations marked the permanent reopening of investigations.

Forgoing tunneling, Maiuri worked methodically from the surface down and held rigorously to the modern practice of leaving as much as possible in place—pots on the stove, a meal on the table, writing tablets carelessly shoved under a bed. As the laborious digging proceeded, the town's character became more apparent, confirming scholars' speculations. Herculaneum had been a quieter, perhaps more culturally inclined community than Pompeii. In addition to the absence of wheel ruts, there were no steppingstones across its avenues, suggesting that they were cleaner and better drained. And there was a distinct upper-class quarter—an elegant waterfront terrace of mansions arranged on different levels, with verandas, porches, and windows offering sweeping views of the bay.

143

The House of the Mosaic Atrium exemplifies the gracious domestic style enjoyed by Herculaneum's wealthy householders. Laid out to take maximum advantage of the sea breezes and vistas, it was effectively two houses in one: an original atrium house (entered through a doorway bearing a mosaic sign reading *Cave canem,* "Beware of the dog"), and a later extension built along the old town wall. The addition incorporated a colonnaded garden with a fountain, a glass-enclosed portico, and a solarium, or sun deck, with a small shaded room at each end, where

In the House of the Gem, shown above with its red-roofed atrium restored, excavators came upon a carbonized wooden cradle holding the skeleton of a baby. The house takes its name from a gemstone, etched with an image of a woman, that was unearthed in the ruins.

the residents could nap during the heat of the day. In its decor and appointments, this house is modest compared with its neighbor, the House of the Stags, so called after two of the statues found in its garden. Built only about 25 years before Vesuvius erupted, it has a spacious, almost modern feel. The traditional garden colonnade was replaced by a windowed corridor decorated with paintings of cupids at play. The owner's mischievous taste in artistic themes was well demonstrated in the garden, with its statues of a drunken satyr hefting a wineskin, and an even drunker Hercules fumbling to urinate. Among the more-everyday items recovered was a set of terra-cotta pots on a charcoal stove. Also found was a bronze bathtub, something of a rarity given the Roman preference for visiting public baths.

As at Pompeii, not every patrician home was occupied by a single wealthy family. By the first century AD, many of the old nobility were living in straitened circumstances, and in all probability some were obliged to subdivide their property to pay for repairs after the earthquake. Such arrangements are apparent at the House of the Wooden Partition, one of the best-preserved residences in the area. Dating from pre-Roman times, it had once been a luxurious domicile stretching over an entire block, but later the rooms fronting the street had been converted into shops and artisans' apartments. In addition, a second story with a separate entrance and stairway was built on, to be either rented or sold outright. However, in their restricted ground-floor quarters, the landlord's family still enjoyed a measure of gracious living, surrounded by fine marbles.

The feature for which the house is named is a set of wooden panels—now carbonized—that were used to close off the tablinum

Carbonized wooden doors that still open on pivots separate an atrium, with its elegant marble table and impluvium, from the rest of the aptly named House of the Wooden Partition. Before 18th-century tunnelers destroyed them, another set of doors filled the gap between the remaining pair.

from the atrium. Of the three sections that formed the partition, two are in such excellent condition that they still turn easily on their pivot pins—testimony to the remarkable preservative powers of the volcanic muck that encased the town. Wooden bedframes also survive in two small rooms near the main entrance, and elsewhere in the house an assortment of everyday objects, from glass jars and perfume flasks to a bronze sewing needle and a straw broom, shed light on the daily existence of the owners. In one room, archaeologists discovered a piece of carbonized bread, torn from a loaf just as Vesuvius exploded, with a piece of tablecloth fused to it.

Another patrician home that had been subdivided contains a mystery. In a small upper room, at the center of a stucco panel, is an unusual mark in the plaster, apparently left after some object was hastily torn from the wall: It looks very much like a Christian cross. Some scholars say that the appearance is deceiving, that these are merely the marks of a shelf. But the mounting nails were driven at the top and bottom of the longer vertical piece—not the sturdiest arrangement—and the shape itself is rather odd for a shelf. Given that the apostle Paul landed at Puteoli, just a few miles west of Neapolis, in AD 61, it is possible that there were Christians in Herculaneum. Whether they were using the cross as a symbol at this early date is in doubt. No one, however, disputes a Jewish presence in the area: At another house nearby, someone has scribbled the Hebraic name *David* on a wall.

For middle-class Herculaneans with money enough to buy their own homes, shortage of building space was a limiting factor. One such dwelling was connected to a cereal shop, but inside the owner displayed his refinement and compensated for the lack of a garden by adorning the dining room with brilliantly colored floral mosaics. Telling domestic details preserved at this site include a list of wine deliveries and their dates written on a wall, and words that a child had scrawled, no doubt for spelling practice.

Less monied families either rented rooms—such as those in a massive apartment block on the sea front—or constructed two-story houses of wood and

Uncovered in the home of a Herculanean gem cutter, a bed fashioned of inlaid wood bears the skeleton of an adolescent boy who may have been too ill to flee when Vesuvius erupted. A re-created embroidery frame and a stool stand next to the bed, where were found chicken bones, the poignant remains of the youth's last meal. The skeleton of a woman—possibly that of the boy's mother or a slave attendant—lay collapsed beside the stool.

This partly restored wooden cabinet (left) functioned as both shrine and closet, with the top portion built in the shape of a temple to hold statuettes of the owners' household gods. The lower section served as a catchall; when opened, it revealed a trove of everyday objects—perfume flasks, buttons, even a dish of garlic.

rubble, with internal walls built of earth- or plaster-coated wood or reeds. In the first century BC, the Roman architect and engineer Vitruvius had condemned such structures as flimsy and unsafe; nevertheless, one example in Herculaneum—next-door to the House of the Wooden Partition—survived the final cataclysm with its furniture and fittings intact. Only 22 feet wide but designed to accommodate two families on the second floor, this house was supplied by a single well from which water was drawn by means of a windlass and rope—recovered in near-original condition.

Equally well preserved were the contents of some of Herculaneum's shops. At one establishment, beans and chickpeas still lay piled on the counter for sale; amphorae of wine stood on an intact wooden scaffold with a small oil lamp hanging underneath, and the stove was loaded with charcoal, ready to be lighted. At the bakery of Sextus Patulcus Felix, whose identity is known from a seal perhaps used to stamp his name into the dough, mixing bowls, 25 bronze baking pans, supplies of wheat, and stacks of coins had been abandoned in the rush for safety. To ensure that his cakes would rise, Patulcus had placed carved phalluses—the standard good-luck charm—over the oven door and in the dough room.

Next to Patulcus' bakery lay a tavern with a fresco of a robed Hercules serving wine to the nude figures of Dionysus and Mercury—who besides being messenger to the gods was also the patron deity of shopkeepers. Here, the storage vessels for wine were laid lengthwise in racks suspended from the ceiling. In one of Herculaneum's wineshops, a patron, possibly in his cups, has scrawled a despondent observation: "To live is vain." In another was this message: "Hyacinthus was here. Salutations to his own Virginia."

Commercial establishments in Herculaneum seem to have been small-scale, perhaps sized to meet local demands (with so little of the town uncovered, however, this picture may eventually change). Fullers were well represented, though not nearly as extensively as at Pompeii. Romans traditionally wore plain white garb, but the fashion in the first century AD was beginning to tend toward patterned materials in bright colors. At the premises of one cloth merchant, a small patch of fabric was discovered, fragile as a spider's web but still showing a wavy pattern. Another prize from Herculaneum was a cloth press recovered from one of the workshops on the ground floor of the House of the Wooden Partition. Operated by a worm screw, the machine is remarkably similar in design to the first printing presses, developed 1,300 years later.

The owners of this familiarly shaped bronze bathtub in the House of the Stags apparently preferred the privacy of their home to the public baths favored by most Romans. The marble bowl on the pedestal also may have been used for ablutions.

With the exception of netmaking businesses that catered to fishermen, other trades in the town paralleled those of Pompeii. In one workshop, a decorator specialized in creating painted wooden panels for the homes of the wealthy. At another, a gem cutter displayed his wares on a marble table. In the back room of this shop, the gem cutter's wife, or perhaps a slave employee, produced embroidery on a loom that had been placed close to a bed veneered with rare woods. It was here that the skeleton of a youth, possibly the invalid son of the gem cutter, was found. Unable to rise from his bed, he perished where he lay, his last meal beside him.

Continuous rows of shops line the main street, which presumably leads to the Forum—still to be located. Of the other public buildings, a palaestra and two baths have been systematically explored under the direction of Giuseppe Maggi, the archaeologist who assumed supervision of excavations in 1971.

For such a modest-sized town, the Palaestra was remarkably large: 360 feet by 260 feet, centered on a cross-shaped swimming pool measuring some 160 feet in one direction and 100 feet in the other. Where the arms intersected stood a huge bronze serpent coiled around the limbs of a tree, water spurting from its five heads. Ordinary spectators watched athletic competitions from a portico running around three sides of the games area, but dignitaries watched from a special box. At a presentation area, the victors' olive wreaths were laid out on a marble table with legs terminating in eagle claws.

Of the two public baths, the older, situated near the presumed center of town, follow a typical Roman design. After working out in a central courtyard, clients might have enjoyed a massage in one of the surrounding chambers before progressing to the warm and then hot steam rooms, finishing up with a cold plunge in the small circular pool at one corner of the building. These so-called Central Baths included separate facilities for men and women.

Whereas the Central Baths were probably paid for by the municipality, the Suburban Baths were apparently another gift of Proconsul Balbus. His statue and a memorial altar once stood in the building, which also gave access to the house thought to be the Balbus home. Judging by the establishment's restrained but luxurious decor and its proximity to the mansions on the waterfront, it was strictly for the well-to-do. The facilities were not segregated, but men and women probably attended at different times of the day, the women in the morning and the men in the afternoon. Despite the apparent air of propriety, trysts were evidently commonplace. Many

A vestibule of the Suburban Baths, frequented only by Herculaneum's wealthy, exemplifies that facility's luxurious modernity. Above double arches on columns that were once a vibrant red, a skylight lets in light over a marble basin equipped with fittings—concealed in the figure of Apollo—for running water.

heterosexual and homosexual encounters are recorded on the walls of a small room. Its use is officially described as unknown, but its function can be inferred from graffiti such as this one: "Two close companions were here, and after the bad guidance of Epaphroditus in everything, they finally threw him out. Then with the girls they joyfully spent 105½ sesterces."

The Suburban Baths held up astoundingly well against the volcanic avalanche that struck early on August 25, AD 79. The fact that the shoreline was pushed nearly half a mile out into the bay indicates that the flow had not lost any of its strength when it reached the baths. The building owes its survival to its construction—walls of brick-faced concrete with vaults supporting the roof. Debris pouring in through a skylight and filling the interior may also have helped by offsetting the pressure from the outside.

Another miraculous instance of preservation lies a short way off. Farther down on the beach, near the spot where the many skeletons were found, diggers in 1982 came upon a boat. It had been carbonized by the heat and was extremely fragile, but its structure was largely intact, with the bronze nails that fixed its timbers still in place. According to J. Richard Steffy, a nautical archaeologist from Texas A & M University who took part in the initial studies, the 26-foot-long craft was most likely a harbor tug or a wine carrier. The sweeping hull—similar to ones featured in wall paintings of the time—and the workmanship seem worthy of a master carpenter. A long tapered timber found close by may be the ship's mast.

Perhaps a few of those who rushed toward the shore in their last moments thought of escaping on this very boat. But it was not to be. A skeleton found nearby still clutched an oar. Just behind the boat, inside one of the storage chambers, 12 victims lay huddled together, most likely members of the same household. Expert analysis of their bones revealed the age and sex of the seven adults: three men, ages 25, 31, and 35; four women, ages 14, 16, 38, and 42; four children, ages 3, 5, 9, and 10; and a seven-month-old baby. Dropped in the sand around them were a few pathetic possessions grabbed before they took flight—a lamp, an iron house key, and, saddest of all, a child's small coin box containing one bronze and one silver coin.

These skeletons and the scores of others found in the chambers along the beach bear mute testimony to the hopelessness of that dreadful day. In their humanity, they bridge the gap between then and now, stirring a desire to learn even more about their lives. At Herculaneum in particular, despite obvious obstacles, the possibilities are tantalizing. With only seven city blocks uncovered and exciting new finds yet to be made—a necropolis, temples, markets, the Forum, and possibly an amphitheater—it seems inevitable that the quest will go on. But no less likely is the chance that fate will intervene in the future as it did long ago. In 1980, an earthquake shook the region, breaking treasured objects in the Naples National Archaeological Museum and inflicting so much damage on the painstakingly cleared ruins of Pompeii that portions of the city had to be closed to the public for several years. Now almost completely reopened, Pompeii, along with Herculaneum, continues to astonish visitors from around the world. But there in the background, dwarfing the structures of both the classical and the modern age, Mount Vesuvius still smokes and, occasionally, rumbles.

AN EYE FOR NATURE

Sweeping expanses of land and sea; creatures of the earth, ocean, and sky; lush gardens teeming with verdure: The Romans loved all of nature and seized any opportunity to surround themselves with its varied wonders. When not basking among the living gifts of the outdoors, they re-created them inside in grand murals and mosaic pavements. Painted directly onto the wall, a garden scene replete with laurel trees, a fountain, and perhaps a nightingale perched in a rose bush (above) could transform a small, windowless bedroom into an oasis of tranquillity. Images of fruit, fish, and fowl might adorn the floor of a *triclinium*, or dining area, not only enchanting the eye but reflecting the room's function as well. Often rendered with near-photographic realism, the creations could almost lead one to imagine birdsong, or stoop to pick up a fallen pear on the tiles.

Working on surfaces of both wet and dry plaster, which had been infused with powdered marble and alabaster for luster and strength, painters achieved a combination of soft effects and vibrant, sharply defined images. Their rich pigments came from all manner of exotic and ordinary sources—mineral, vegetable, and animal. These included ochers, malachite, and cinnabar for certain yellows, greens, and reds; plants of the genus *Indigofera* for blue; and sea mollusks for the brilliant and expensive Tyrian purple, to name but a few. Studio artisans, piecing together countless *tesserae*—tiny chips of stone, marble, and colored glass—in terra-cotta trays later set in floors, crafted the finer mosaics by emulating the styles and themes of painted masterpieces.

Entombed—and preserved—under Vesuvian ash, the murals of Pompeii and its near neighbors endured the passing centuries with much of their vividness intact. Along with the beautiful mosaics discovered with them, the paintings reveal nature's place in the hearts of the people of Pompeii and the immortality the artists bestowed on their living subjects.

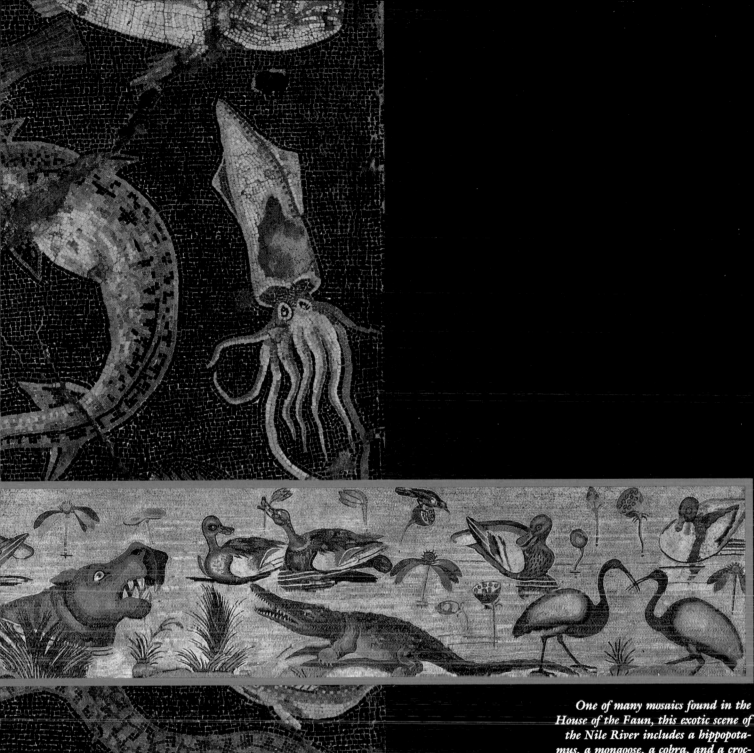

One of many mosaics found in the House of the Faun, this exotic scene of the Nile River includes a hippopotamus, a mongoose, a cobra, and a crocodile. Egyptian images and themes appeared frequently in Roman art.

Squid, bass, eel, and other marine creatures—all found in the Bay of Naples—swarm about a lobster ensnared in octopus tentacles. Like most figure mosaics, this three-foot-square emblema, or panel, was assembled by studio artisans and then added to a larger, less intricate pavement.

Herons—much admired by the Romans—can be seen in many garden paintings. At right, a heron perches between flowering oleander and white-blossomed myrtle, while a song thrush peers down from a stylized pine.

In a detail from a large room covered with paintings of plants and birds, a purple swamp hen—a species that abounded during the time of the empire but has since disappeared from the area—struts among laurel, violets, and chamomile (below). At left, from a villa north of Pompeii, a wryneck (a bird of the woodpecker family) inspects a trio of pears on a trompe l'oeil shelf.

In a two-part mosaic from a back room of the House of the Faun, a domestic cat attacks a partridge; below, two colorful ducks are grouped in a still life with birds, fish, and shellfish ready for cooking.

Two angry-eyed fighting cocks spar to the death before a table with a betting purse on top of it in this mosaic, a vivid example of Roman depictions of nature's cruelty figure heavily in Roman depictions of animal and sea life.

Oleander, myrtle, and roses bloom around a bowl-shaped fountain—perhaps a birdbath for the swallows, song thrushes, golden orioles, and shrikes that frequented Pompeian gardens. The painted lattice and background shrubbery create an illusion of depth in this wall painting in the peristyle of the House of Venus Marina.

In the bedroom of a house probably owned by a Pompeian fruit cultivator, cherry, plum, pear, pomegranate, and lemon trees climb the walls behind golden fences; several birds light on the branches, while a serpent slithers up the fig tree at center.

TWO CITIES IN HISTORY'S SHADOW

From their misty origins near the turn of the first millennium BC until their sudden extinction in AD 79, Pompeii and Herculaneum enjoyed a relatively unremarkable history as the world around them underwent tumultuous change. Their idyllic setting on the sunny flanks of Mount Vesuvius, by the Bay of Naples, provided a pleasant life for the inhabitants and attracted a fair share of famous visitors and temporary residents. In all their centuries, however, the two communities produced no great figures of their own, saw no great battles, commanded no great wealth. Yet in the manner of their passing, and in the miraculous state of their preservation, they have become among the most famous and important sites of the entire classical period. The timeline on these pages traces Pompeii and Herculaneum from what little is known of their earliest settlement to their final years as part of the Roman Empire. Because the cities were such minor players in their own time, larger events elsewhere in the Mediterranean world are included as points of reference.

Legend has it that Herculaneum was established by its namesake, Hercules. Scholars believe both towns, in fact, had mundane origins, arising from small villages of the Oscans, an indigenous tribal group. Pompeii, settled possibly as early as 1000 BC, may derive its name from the Oscan word for "five," although the reasons are not clear. The Etruscans founded nearby Capua before 600 BC, and Greeks soon colonized Ischia, in the Bay of Naples; these two peoples and the Samnites, a fierce clan from the mountainous interior, vied for dominance in the region for several centuries. Meanwhile, to the north, Rome emerged—founded, tradition says, in 753 BC by Romulus and Remus, brothers suckled in infancy by a wolf (below).

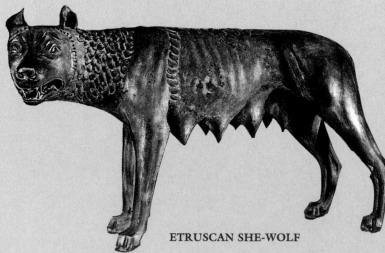

ETRUSCAN SHE-WOLF

EARLY ROMAN REPUBLIC
509-133 BC

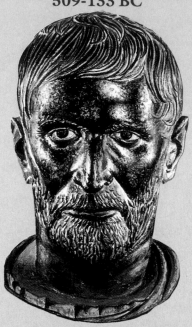

LUCIUS JUNIUS BRUTUS

509 The Roman Republic is founded; Lucius Junius Brutus and Lucius Tarquinius Collatinus are its first consuls. The bronze bust above was long thought to represent Brutus, but scholars now have doubts about this.

508 Rome elects its first magistrates.

494 Roman plebeians begin the Struggle of the Orders, demanding full political equality with the ruling patricians.

ca. 475-420 Greek influence increases at Pompeii.

451 Rome's first written laws are published.

447-432 In Athens, the Greeks build the Parthenon.

ca. 425-375 Samnites enlarge the old city at Pompeii.

390 Rome is sacked by invading Gauls.

367 The Struggle of the Orders ends as plebeians win the right to serve as consuls.

343-290 Samnite wars rage near Pompeii; Rome intervenes, taking Pompeii as an ally. The city's walls are rebuilt with limestone from the Sarno River.

333-323 Alexander the Great conquers the Persian Empire.

264 The earliest recorded gladiatorial combat takes place.

264-241 In an era of expansion, Rome defeats Carthage in the First Punic War, annexing Sicily, Sardinia, and Corsica.

218-201 In the Second Punic War, Carthage becomes a Roman protectorate and gives up its possessions in Spain. Pompeii's walls are rebuilt of tufa from nearby Nuceria.

200-133 Rome fights wars in Spain, Greece, Macedonia, Asia Minor, and North Syria, conquering Spain, Greece, and Macedonia and destroying Carthage and Corinth. Sicilian slaves revolt in 135 BC.

PERIOD OF ROMAN REVOLUTION
133–31 BC

JULIUS CAESAR

133 Tribune Tiberius Gracchus challenges the authority of the Roman Senate; he tries to institute land reforms and is murdered.
ca. 125 Pompeians build the Basilica and the large theater.
91-88 Rome fights the so-called Social War against Italian allies, including Pompeii. Soldiers slaughter the Samnite nobility.
ca. 88 Pompeii is made a *municipium*—a provincial town dependent on Rome—and its inhabitants become Roman citizens.
81-79 Lucius Cornelius Sulla, a general, becomes dictator at Rome; he rewrites the constitution to renew the Senate's control of the state.
80-70 Pompeii builds its Amphitheater.
ca. 80 Latin becomes the official language at Pompeii, Roman weights and measures are introduced, and the town constitution is Romanized. To punish Pompeians for their part in the Social War, Publius Cornelius Sulla, nephew of Lucius, confiscates land and awards it to 5,000 of his uncle's veterans. In the succeeding decades, Pompeii's new Roman population and its older Samnite, Oscan, and Greek peoples intermarry.
73-71 On and near Vesuvius, Spartacus leads 70,000 of his fellow slaves in a revolt that ultimately fails.
70 Pompey and Crassus are elected consuls of Rome.
63 Cicero becomes consul.
60 Julius Caesar, Pompey, and Crassus form the First Triumvirate.
49-44 The Roman Republic is torn by civil war. In 44 BC, Caesar is made dictator for life; he is assassinated on March 15 by a group that includes Marcus Junius Brutus, a reputed descendant of founding father Lucius Junius Brutus.
44-31 Civil war rages among Caesar's political heirs—Antony, Lepidus, and Octavian (later called Augustus).

EARLY ROMAN EMPIRE
31 BC–AD 79

AUGUSTUS

31 BC Octavian, Caesar's grandnephew, wins the battle of Actium, defeating Antony and Cleopatra, queen of Egypt and Caesar's former mistress.
31-27 Octavian reorganizes the Roman state and receives the title of Augustus.
27 BC-AD 14 Augustus reigns as emperor, turning over Roman provinces without armies to the Senate's care, and using the armies under his command to garrison more remote areas such as Spain, Gaul, and Syria. In Pompeii, the large theater is rebuilt and a new Basilica constructed; Augustus is honored with the Temple of Fortuna Augusta.
14-37 Tiberius reigns.
ca. 33 Jesus of Nazareth is crucified in Jerusalem.
37 Caligula becomes emperor; he later serves as one of Pompeii's chief magistrates.
41 Claudius succeeds Caligula and rules for 13 years.
43-48 Claudius begins the conquest of Britain.
54-68 Nero, the last of the Julio-Claudian dynasty, rules.
59 The Pompeians battle their local rivals, the Nucerians, in Pompeii's Amphitheater, and Nero demands that the Amphitheater be closed for 10 years.
62 On February 5, an earthquake devastates Pompeii and Herculaneum.
69-81 After a brief period of civil war, Vespasian comes to power. During his reign and that of his son Titus, Rome and the empire are reconstructed politically, militarily, and financially.
70 Titus destroys the temple in Jerusalem.
79 On August 24 and 25, Vesuvius erupts, burying Pompeii, Herculaneum, and outlying districts.

ACKNOWLEDGMENTS

The editors wish to thank the following individuals and institutions for their valuable assistance in the preparation of this volume: Margaret Alexander, University of Iowa, Iowa City; Giulia Aurigemma, Rome; Brigitte Baumbusch, Florence; Donatella Bertoni, Milan; Jane Bisel, Rochester, Minnesota; Horst Blanck, Istituto Archeologico Germanico, Rome; Stefano Bruschini, IBM Semea, Rome; Steven Carey, University of Rhode Island, Narragansett; Robert I. Curtis, University of Georgia, Athens; Stefano De Caro, Soprintendente, Maria Rosaria Esposito, Chiara Lepore, Maria Grazia Ruggi d'Aragona, Valeria Sanpaolo, Soprintendenza Archeologica di Napoli, Naples; Baldassare Conticello, Soprintendente, Antonio D'Ambrosio, Ernesto De Carolis, Maria De Conte, Lorenzo Fergola, Salvatore Ciro Nappo, Mario Pagano, Antonio Varone, Soprintendenza Archeologica di Pompei, Pompeii; Joseph Jay Deiss, Gainesville, Florida; Helmut Jung, Istituto Archeologico Germanico, Rome; Maria Montembault, Documentaliste, Département des Antiquités Grecques et Romaines, Musée du Louvre, Paris; Margaret Somerville Roberts, Philadelphia, Pennsylvania.

PICTURE CREDITS

stroyed by Vesuvius by Wilhelmina F. Jashemski, Caratzas Brothers, New Rochelle, N.Y., 1979. 104, 105: Background Erich Lessing/Culture and Fine Arts Archive, Vienna. Alfredo and Pio Foglia, Naples (2). 106, 107: Alfredo and Pio Foglia, Naples; Alinari, Florence; Alfredo and Pio Foglia, Naples. 108, 109: Metropolitan Museum of Art, Rogers Fund, 1903 (03.14.13) detail #7. 111: Mario De Biasi/Mondadori, Milan. 112-116: Antonia Mulas, Milan. 117: Mimmo Jodice, Naples. 118: Josef Adamiak, Leipzig. 119: ©Leonard von Matt/Photo Researchers. 120, 121: Stan Goldberg Assoc. Inc./Superstock. 122, 123: Werner Forman Archive, London. 124, 125: Alfredo and Pio Foglia, Naples. 126-128: Mimmo Jodice, Naples. 129: From Hercula-

neum: Italy's Buried Treasure by Joseph Jay Deiss, revised and updated edition published by the J. Paul Getty Museum, Malibu, Calif., 1989. 130, 131: ©Leonard von Matt/Photo Researchers. 133: Courtesy Sara Bisel—Joe McNally. 134: Courtesy Sara Bisel—by O. Louis Mazzatenta, ©National Geographic Society. 135: By O. Louis Mazzatenta, ©National Geographic Society—courtesy Sara Bisel. 136: Courtesy Sara Bisel except lower right, Jonathan Blair/Woodfin Camp and Associates. 137: Courtesy Sara Bisel—Jonathan Blair/Woodfin Camp and Associates. 138: Map from "La Villa Ercolanese dei Pisoni" by Domenico Comparetti and Guilio De Petra, Ermanno Loescher, Turin, 1883. 139: J. Paul Getty Museum, Malibu, Calif., main peristyle garden

and fountain. 140, 141: Luciano Pedicini, Naples/Biblioteca Nazionale, Naples. 142: Alfredo and Pio Foglia, Naples. 144: Mimmo Jodice, Naples. 145: C. Bevilacqua/IGDA, Milan. 146, 147: Soprintendenza Archeologica di Pompei, Pompeii. 148, 149: Mimmo Jodice, Naples. 151: Alfredo and Pio Foglia, Naples. 152, 153: Mimmo Jodice, Naples. 154: Mimmo Jodice, Naples—Alfredo and Pio Foglia, Naples. 155: Stanley A. Jashemski, from The Gardens of Pompeii, Herculaneum and the Villas Destroyed by Vesuvius by Wilhelmina F. Jashemski, Caratzas Brothers, New Rochelle, N.Y., 1979. 156, 157: Photo Nimatallah/ARTEPHOT, Paris; Mimmo Jodice, Naples. 158, 159: Mimmo Jodice, Naples. 160, 161: Art by Paul Breeden.

BIBLIOGRAPHY

BOOKS

Ackerman, James S. The Villa. Princeton, N.J.: Princeton University Press, 1990.

Adams, W. H. Davenport. The Buried Cities of Campania. London: Thomas Nelson, 1868.

Andrews, Ian. Pompeii (Cambridge Introduction to World History series, edited by Trevor Cairns). New York: Cambridge University Press, 1978.

Arnott, Peter D. The Romans and Their World. New York: St. Martin's Press, 1970.

Bieber, Margarete. The History of the Greek and Roman Theater. Princeton, N.J.: Princeton University Press, 1961.

Bisel, Sara. "Human Bones at Herculaneum." In Vol. 1 of Rivista di Studi Pompeiani. Rome: L'Erma di Bretschneider, 1987.

Bisel, Sara C., with Jane Bisel and Shelley Tanaka. The Secrets of Vesuvius. Toronto: Madison Press, 1990.

Brilliant, Richard. Pompeii AD 79. New York: Clarkson N. Potter, 1979.

Brion, Marcel. Pompeii and Herculaneum. Translated by John Rosenberg. New York: Crown Publishers, 1960.

Castronuovo, Sandro, and Vincenzo Litta. The Papyrii of Herculaneum. Translated by Zinnia M. Steinhauer. Naples: Naples Tourist Board, n.d.

Ceram, C. W. A Picture History of Archaeology. London: Thames and Hudson, 1959.

Ceram, C. W. (Ed.). Hands on the Past. New York: Alfred A. Knopf, 1966.

Clarke, M. L. The Roman Mind: Studies in the History of Thought from Cicero to Marcus Aurelius. New York: W. W. Norton, 1968.

Connolly, Peter. Pompeii. London: Macdonald Educational, 1979.

Corbett, Patricia. Roman Art. New York: Avenel Books, 1980.

Corbishley, Mike. The Roman World. New York: Warwick Press, 1986.

Curtis, Robert I. (Ed.). Pompeiana (Vol. 1 of Studia Pompeiana et Classica: In Honor of Wilhelmina F. Jashemski). New Rochelle, N.Y.: Orpheus Publishing, 1989.

D'Arms, John H. Romans on the Bay of Naples. Cambridge, Mass.: Harvard University Press, 1970.

D'Avino, Michele. The Women of Pompeii. Translated by Monica Hope Jones and Luigi Nusco. Naples: Loffredo, 1967.

De Franciscis, Alfonso. The Buried Cities. New York: Crescent Books, 1978.

Deiss, Joseph Jay. Herculaneum (rev. ed.). Malibu, Calif.: J. Paul Getty Museum, 1989.

de Simone, Antonio. "The History, Topography, and Urban Development of Pompeii." In Pompeii and Its Museums (Great Museums of the World series, Henry A. La Farge, editorial director). Milan: Newsweek and Arnoldo Mondadori Editore, 1979.

Empires Ascendant: TimeFrame 400 BC-AD 200 (Time Frame series). Alexandria, Va.: Time-Life Books, 1987.

Eschebach, Hans. Pompeji. Leipzig: VEB E. A. Seemann, 1978.

Étienne, Robert. Pompéi: La Cité Ensevelie. Paris: Gallimard, 1987.

Fischer, Peter. Mosaic. New York: McGraw-Hill, 1971.

Flower, Barbara, and Elisabeth Rosenbaum (Trans.). *The Roman Cookery Book*. London: Peter Nevill, 1958.

Franklin, James L., Jr. *Pompeii: The Electoral Programmata, Campaigns and Politics, A.D. 71-79*. Rome: American Academy, 1980.

From Pagan Rome to Byzantium (Vol. 1 of *A History of Private Life*, edited by Paul Veyne and translated by Arthur Goldhammer). Cambridge, Mass.: Harvard University Press, 1987.

Goodenough, Simon. *Citizens of Rome*. New York: Crown Publishers, 1979.

Goor, Ron, and Nancy Goor. *Pompeii*. New York: Thomas Y. Crowell, 1986.

Grant, Michael:
Cities of Vesuvius. New York: Macmillan, 1971.
Time Stopped at Pompeii (Chap. 6 of *Discovery of Lost Worlds*, edited by Joseph J. Thorndike, Jr.). New York: American Heritage Publishing, 1979.

Grimal, Pierre. *In Search of Ancient Italy*. Translated by P. D. Cummins. New York: Hill and Wang, 1964.

Hamblin, Dora Jane. *Pots and Robbers*. New York: Simon and Schuster, 1970.

Heintze, Helga von. *Roman Art*. New York: Universe Books, 1979.

Henig, Martin (Ed.). *A Handbook of Roman Art*. Ithaca, N.Y.: Cornell University Press, 1983.

James, Simon. *Ancient Rome*. New York: Alfred A. Knopf, 1990.

Jashemski, Wilhelmina F. *The Gardens of Pompeii, Herculaneum and the Villas Destroyed by Vesuvius*. New Rochelle, N.Y.: Caratzas Brothers, 1979.

Kraus, Theodor. *Pompeii and Herculaneum*. Translated by Robert Erich Wolf. New York: Harry N. Abrams, 1975.

Ling, Roger:
"The Arts of Living." In *The Oxford History of the Classical World*, edited by John Boardman, Jasper Griffin, and Oswyn Murray. Oxford: Oxford University Press, 1986.
Roman Painting. New York: Cambridge University Press, 1991.

Lyttelton, Margaret, and Werner Forman. *The Romans*. London: Orbis Publishing, 1984.

MacKendrick, Paul. *The Mute Stones Speak* (2d ed.). New York: W. W. Norton, 1960.

Maggi, Giuseppe. *Ercolano*. Naples: Loffredo, 1985.

Massa, Aldo. *The World of Pompeii*. Translated by David McDougall. Geneva: Editions Minerva, 1972.

Mau, August. *Pompeii: Its Life and Art*. Translated by Francis W. Kelsey. New Rochelle, N.Y.: Caratzas Brothers, 1982.

Mayeske, Betty Jo. "A Pompeian Bakery on the Via dell'Abbondanza." In *Pompeiana* (Vol. 1 of *Studia Pompeiana et Classica: In Honor of Wilhelmina F. Jashemski*, edited by Robert I. Curtis). New Rochelle, N.Y.: Orpheus Publishing, 1989.

National Geographic Society. *Splendors of the Past: Lost Cities of the Ancient World*. Washington, D.C.: National Geographic Society, 1981.

Perring, Stefania, and Dominic Perring. *Then and Now*. New York: Macmillan, 1991.

Picard, Gilbert. *Roman Painting* (Vol. 4 of *The Pallas Library of Art*). Greenwich, Conn.: New York Graphic Society, 1968.

Pompeii and Its Museums (Great Museums of the World series, Henry A. La Farge, editorial director). Milan: Newsweek and Arnoldo Mondadori Editore, 1979.

Pucci, Eugenio. *New Practical Guide of Pompeii*. Florence: Bonechi, 1992.

Researches in Campanian Archaeology (RICA). *Cartography* (Part 5 of *Corpus Topographicum Pompeianum*). Austin: University of Texas at Austin, 1981.

Richardson, Lawrence, Jr. *Pompeii*. Baltimore: Johns Hopkins University Press, 1988.

The Roman World (Vol. 2 of *The Oxford History of the Classical World*, edited by John Boardman, Jasper Griffin, and Oswyn Murray). Oxford: Oxford University Press, 1989.

Scarborough, John. *Roman Medicine*. London: Thames and Hudson, 1969.

Sear, Frank. *Roman Architecture*. Ithaca, N.Y.: Cornell University Press, 1982.

Shelton, Jo-Ann. *As the Romans Did*. New York: Oxford University Press, 1988.

Stambaugh, John E. *The Ancient Roman City*. Baltimore: Johns Hopkins University Press, 1988.

Starr, Chester G. *The Ancient Romans*. New York: Oxford University Press, 1971.

Strong, Donald, and David Brown (Eds.). *Roman Crafts*. New York: New York University Press, 1976.

Trevelyan, Raleigh. *The Shadow of Vesuvius*. London: Michael Joseph, 1976.

Vanags, Patricia. *The Glory That Was Pompeii*. New York: Mayflower Books, n.d.

Vehling, Joseph Dommers (Trans.). *Apicius: Cookery and Dining in Ancient Rome*. New York: Dover Publications, 1977.

Volcano (Planet Earth series). Alexandria, Va.: Time-Life Books, 1987.

Walker, Susan. *Roman Art*. London: British Museum Press, 1991.

Ward, Anne. *Adventures in Archaeology*. New York: Larousse, 1977.

Ward-Perkins, John, and Amanda Claridge. *Pompeii A.D. 79*. New York: Alfred A. Knopf, 1978.

Wheeler, Margaret. *History Was Buried*. New York: Galahad Books, 1967.

Wheeler, Mortimer. *Roman Art and Architecture*. London: Thames and Hudson, 1964.

Woodford, Susan. *The Art of Greece and Rome*. Cambridge: Cambridge University Press, 1982.

PERIODICALS

Brownlee, Shannon. "Sara Bisel, the Bone Lady." *Discover,* October 1984.

"Eight More Huddled Bodies Found in Pompeii's Ruins." *New York Times,* August 30, 1991.

Evans, Edith. "Dining with the Ancients." *Archaeology,* November/December 1990.

Gore, Rick. "The Dead Do Tell Tales at Vesuvius." *National Geographic,* May 1984.

Gore, Rick, and O. L. Massatenta. "Biography by Bones." *National Geographic,* May 1984.

Judge, Joseph. "A Buried Roman Town Gives Up Its Dead." *National*

Geographic, December 1982.

Maiuri, Amedeo, Peter V. Bianchi, and Lee E. Battaglia. "Last Moments of the Pompeians." *National Geographic,* November 1961.

Rondinone, Peter, and Kathrine Jason. "Ruining Herculaneum." *Omni,* August 1984.

Schiller, Ronald. "The City Where Time Stood Still." *Reader's Digest,* December 1986.

Sigurdsson, Haraldur, et al. "The Eruption of Vesuvius in A.D. 79." *National Geographic Research,* Vol. 1, no. 3, Summer 1985.

"The Victims of Mount Vesuvius." *Newsweek,* November 29, 1982.

OTHER SOURCES

Anderson, Maxwell L. "Pompeian Frescoes in the Metropolitan Museum of Art." Reprinted from the *Metropolitan Museum of Art Bulletin,* Winter 1987/88.

J. Paul Getty Museum. *Guide to the Villa and Its Gardens.* Malibu, Calif.: J. Paul Getty Museum, 1989.

Le Collezioni del Museo Nazionale di Napoli. Catalog from the Naples Museum. Rome: De Luca, 1986.

Le Collezioni del Museo Nazionale di Napoli. Catalog from the Naples Museum. Rome: De Luca, 1989.

Rediscovering Pompeii. Catalog of exhibition by IBM-Italia, New York City, IBM Gallery of Science and Art, 12 July-15 September 1990. Rome: L'Erma di Bretschneider, 1990.

MUSEUMS

Readers interested in viewing objects from Pompeii and Herculaneum will find outstanding collections in the following institutions.

Antiquarium, Boscoreale

Antiquarium di Stabiae, Castellammare di Stabia

Biblioteca Nazionale Vittorio Emanuele III, Officina Papiri Ercolanesi, Naples

British Museum, London

J. Paul Getty Museum, Classical Collections, Malibu, California

Metropolitan Museum of Art, New York

Museo Archeologico Nazionale, Naples

Villa di Poppeia, Oplontis, Torre Annunziata

INDEX

and excavated portions of, *map* 46; perfumeries in, 102, 103; plaster casts of victims in, *8, 11,* 33-34, *35, 38-43,* 71; population of, 10, 68; prominence of, 126; public baths in, 48, 65-66, *67,* 104; rediscovery of, 26-27, 127; ruins further damaged in World War II, 68, 80; skeletons found at, *36-37,* 45-46; Social War, 12, 49, 161; sudden destruction and preservation of provides witness to Roman daily life, 7, 11, 32-33, 46-48; taverns in, 16, 64-65; timeline, 160-161; tombs in, 23, 70; typical kitchen in, *92;* villas nearby, 132; walls of, 49-51; water supply for, 105, 113

Pompeii, Its Life and Art (Mau): 47
Pompey the Great: 27, 161
Poppaea: 86
Poppaeus, Quintus: house of, 34
Porcius: and construction of Pompeii's amphitheater, 69
Priapus (deity): 65
Primigenia, Novellia: 86
Proculus, Publius Paquius: house of, 34
Prostitution: 99; and public baths, 149; and taverns, 65
Puteoli: 146

R

Reliefs: *See* Art
Religion: deities, 16, 60, 65, 71-83, 105, 138; religious life in Pompeii and Herculaneum, 63, *71-83,* 130, 146, 147; temples and altars, 2, 16, 60, *61,* 64, *72-79,* 73, 76, 80, 82
Remus: 160
Resina (Ercolano): 26, 143; opposition of residents to excavations at Herculaneum, 127, 129, 142
Resting Hermes: 138
Richardson, Lawrence: 100
Rome: 10, 49, 108; domination of Italian peninsula by, 12, 49; mythical background for, 55, 110, *160;* timeline, 160-161
Romulus: 160
Rothschild, Edmond de: donates Pisasanella silver to Louvre, 90
Royal Society of London: and papyri scrolls from Herculaneum, 139

S

Sabazius (deity): 82; statue of, *83*
Samnites: 12, 51, 160
Sarno River: 12, 26, 46, 48, 49
Satrii family: 87, 88, 95

Scaurus, Aulus Umbricius: 95-97
Seneca: 20, 68; on the earthquake at Pompeii, 17
Silenus: statue of, *106-107,* 132-138
Slaves: 66, 134; manumission of, 93, 97; as tutors, 110
Social War: and Pompeii, 12, 49, 161
Spartacus: 12, 161
Spinazzola, Vittorio: *31;* excavations at Pompeii, *30-31,* 52-53; innovative techniques of, 52-53
Stabiae: 10, 20, 22, 24; and eruption at Vesuvius, *18-19*
Stabian Baths: 65-66
Stabian Gate: 49, 51
Statius: on the fate of Pompeii, 24
Statues: *See* Art
Steffy, J. Richard: and excavation of boat found at Herculaneum, 150
Stoicism: 138
Strabo: 131; on Herculaneum, 126-127
Stromboli: 17
Suburban Baths: 125-126, 149; vestibule of, *149*
Sulla, Lucius Cornelius: 12, 49, 74, 161
Sulla, Publius Cornelius: 87, 161
Synistor, Publius Fannius: house of, *108-109*

T

Tacitus: 68; and Pliny the Younger's account of eruption of Vesuvius, 19
Tanneries: ruins of, 11
Taverns: 16, 64-65
Temple of Apollo: 2, 51, 60, 64, *74-75*
Temple of Bacchus: 80
Temple of Fortuna Augusta: *51,* 161
Temple of Isis: *78-79;* statues from, *79*
Temple of Jupiter: 16, 51, 60, *61,* 72-73
Temple of the Lares: 76
Temple of Venus: *74*
Temple of Vespasian: 72
Texas A & M University: 150
Theater (Herculaneum): 26, 128-129
Theater (Pompeii): 16, 56, *57,* 64, 128, 161
Theaters: masks used in, *56, 59;* satyr plays, *58;* stage set for, *57;* terracotta statue of actor, *59*
Thermopolium: earthenware jars and scales from, *52,* 54
Tiberius: 161; property on Bay of Naples, 13
Titus: 161; and plans to attempt re-

building of Pompeii, 24
Torre Annunziata: 27

U

University of London: 102

V

Valenciennes, Pierre-Henri de: painting by, *18-19*
Valgus: and construction of Pompeii's amphitheater, 69
Vatican: and restoration of papyri found at Herculaneum, 139
Venus (deity): 74
Vespasian: 72, 161
Vesuvius: *cover, end paper, 6-7,* 12, *14-15,* 25, 46, 48, 65, 70, 102, 110, 150, 160; damage from eruption, *map* 12-13; dormant history of, 17; eruption of, 9, 11, 19-23, 71, 76, 98, 104, 129, 144, 146, 149, 161; later eruptions of, 24-25
Vesuvius Gate: 49, 51
Via Consolare: 51
Via dell'Abbondanza: *14-15, 30,* 31, 54, 55, 63, 64, 65, 71, 82, 98; reconstruction project at, 30, 52-53
Via della Fortuna: *50-51*
Via di Nola: 52
Via Mercurio: 63
Via Stabiana: 51, 52, 65, 97, 98
Victor Emmanuel II: and excavations at Pompeii, 28-32
Villa of the Mysteries: bedroom at, *116*
Villa of the Papyri: 141, 142; excavation of, 132-138; floor plan of, 132, *138;* as model for J. Paul Getty Museum, *139,* 142
Villa Pisanella: silverware of, *90-91*
Virgil: 62, 140
Vitruvius: 68, 146-147
Vulcanello: 17
Vulcano: 17

W

Weber, Karl: 142; excavations at Herculaneum, 131-132; and floor plan of the Villa of the Papyri, 132, 138
Winckelmann, Johann Joachim: *26,* 29, 140, 141; on Paderni, 139; study of artifacts from Herculaneum and Pompeii, 28, 129
Wine: 94, 95; utensils for, *23, 90, 94,* 147
Wool-working shops: 11, 62-63

Z

Zeno of Sidon: 138

Neapolis

HERCULES

Herculaneum

BAY OF NAPLES

Rome

VIA APPIA

Pompeii

0   100   200 miles

MEDITERRANEAN SEA